STORM OF ENCHANTED DREAMS
a poetic fairytale
(second edition)

Amanda L. Ball

Storm of Enchanted Dreams
a poetic fairytale

Written and Published by
Amanda L. Ball

Second Edition
Paperback ISBN: 979-8-9922822-6-9
Hardcover ISBN: 979-8-9922822-7-6
eBook ISBN: 979-8-9922822-8-3

For permission requests, please contact the author at:
contact@digitalmedleys.com

Book cover image illustrated by Fiverr designer
Full book cover designed by Amanda L. Ball

• • •

For more content, follow the author's work on social media:
@echoendlessmind

https://digitalmedleys.com

This collection is for my Granny, who always believed in my poetry; I miss you every day.

• • •

For the women who were once little girls with big dreams.

• • •

For Shel who has inspired me since I was five. And for all the poets out there who pour their heart out through words in ink.

May you always have enchanted dreams.

I want my words to stab you in the heart,
aching, pain pouring onto the floor.
And then I want them to stitch you
back up once more.

• • •

The poet does not write to make a living;
the poet writes to feed the soul.

• • •

I was raised on Shel Silverstein; of course I love to rhyme.

• • •

There are no rules in poetry. ♡

Table of Contents

Dear Reader,
(an updated introduction)

I first published *Storm of Enchanted Dreams: a poetic fairytale* in January 2025, which was a compilation of poetry weaving a story of a transition, or awakening of sorts. I guided my readers along my own path as we dodged obstacles, heartbreak, injustice, and eventually found our power to fight back against the enemies in our wake. And this updated second edition is intended to give you a sneak peek into who that woman is transforming into today.

I wrote and published my first two books with my soul dog by my side. Only two months after publishing the second book, he was no longer here. I lost myself again for a while, as he was my true hero. It took some time to grieve, but I finally remembered all of those dreams that fueled me when I was just a girl. It is not fair for me to keep my magic tucked away inside, and so I am here to spread a little more.

While my writing style has always been inspired by stories and fables I read as a child, I write with intention for the strong, witchy, women who deserve to feel that same magic. Please, do not let the world dull your spark. We need you now more than ever.

Take care of yourself as you take this journey with me. It is my hope that as you read the last words, you feel inspired and hopeful after fighting and healing through the chaos.

I am but a writer and these words are my art. I promise there is a happy ending.

May these words enchant you,

♡ Amanda

Storm of Enchanted Dreams

Trigger Warning:
There are some words and thoughts scattered throughout this book that may bring up a lot of hurt and pain and trigger your own memories and grief from the past or present. There are thoughts on mental health issues, anger, pain, social injustice, and revenge seeping through these pages. Though I do not condone violence, I must understand when the oppressed choose to fight back against their oppressors. I encourage each of you to find a healthy way to manage your anger, pain, and grief. Writing has always helped me.

Please take care of yourself while you read these words, and always remember, there is no healing without the chaos of the storm. ♡

• • •

To the women—Trans, Gay, Nonbinary—and to the men who are on our side,
may we never lose hope in a better tomorrow; may we never stop the awakening.

Her Story

•••

Chapter One:
She's quiet and shy
and wants to please.
"All A's Daddy!
Aren't you proud of me?"
She says yes and
rarely argues;
she just wants to be liked.
She tries to be the
perfect child,
she doesn't want a fight.

Chapter Two:
She's angry now,
something's changed.
Mother doesn't know
what to do.
She lost the first man
she ever loved;
she lost a bit of
herself too.
She wants to be different.
She wants to stand out.
She doesn't want to whisper,
she wants to speak loud.
She has a voice she kept in too long,
now it's fueled by loss and anger.
No more shy, quiet girl.
She refuses to bow to any
person or stranger.

Chapter Three:
It took lots of work,
but she made it, she sailed.
She doesn't speak of the times
she almost failed.
She walked the stage,
she wore the cap and gown.
No one knew she almost
drowned.

The man who loved her first
and most,
he was there, and on her
he would boast.
But shortly after, she'd
lose him too.
She held his hand, said,
"I love you"
and watched him slip through.

Chapter Four:
The girl is still
very young,
but life hasn't been easy so far,
and not even that fun.
The girl decides it's time
to take control,
to make big choices,
to start on new goals.
She works many jobs
and makes many friends.
She's labeled as "saucy"
and she doesn't mind
using men.
She has learned to
make her own way,
but she still loves game shows
with Granny…
until the next worst day.
The keeper of secrets,
her very first friend,
slipped away quietly
and nothing makes sense.
A new chapter is here,
there's nothing she can do.
A tear rolls down as
she says, "I'll miss you."

Chapter Five:
She never imagined
she'd be where she is.
Sailing the sky,
having so many adventures.

They call her "lucky"
but oh, she worked hard.
She made it happen,
the victory is hers.
This is the chapter
in which so many friends
come…and they go…
and the loss never ends.
You see, as she's changing,
others are not; or maybe
they are, but their path isn't hers.
It hurts to say goodbye
to so many she has loved.

Chapter Six:
Now the story
is slowing down.
She sold her home.
She left her town.
She said more goodbyes
knowing everything would change,
not knowing who she
would see again.
Life is different.
Her health slowed down.
She doesn't feel so "lucky";
some days she almost drowns.
Starting fresh is her
bravest act yet.
Some days she's ecstatic,
other days she's scared.
But a life without change
is the life that she fears.
So she puts herself out there,
cautious of the next loss;
with unwavering adventure,
she will create the next chapter
no matter the cost.

To be continued…

The Storm is Brewing.

A Chaotic Mind

•••

In the haze,
a chaotic state,
my mind is swirling
between love and hate.
My thoughts have horns,
my thoughts have wings,
they circle, they dive,
they stab, they sting.
The thoughts of trauma,
of pain, of love;
the memories of loss,
of struggles I have shoved
into the back of my eyes,
sitting inside
my chaotic mind.

I laugh, I cry,
I rejoice, I lie
to myself…
to protect the
little girl inside,
hiding within
a chaotic mind.

The love that's lost,
the strains that linger,
the hopes that plummeted,
the ties that were severed.
The dreams I awoke from
that I wanted to remain in…
wishing to go back to
the moments I felt loved in.

The empath mourns,
the anger is real.
I don't have to live it
to feel what they feel.
The passion for
those left behind
stirs up inside
my chaotic mind.

I fight for love.
I fight for hope.
I fight for the voiceless,
as a way to cope.
It's easier to fight
for them
than to confront
my own mind again.

My words are born
from stories I have lived,
from battles I have fought,
from the love I have been
for others who
I still have to forgive.

It would be easier
to let them drown,
these thoughts inside
my chaotic crown.
It would weigh less
if I allowed them to leave,
to not live in me,
to set me free.

But if I were to lose my
words,
to lose my stories,
to lose my hurt,
to lose my worries,
then I may lose
the warrior in me,
the one whose love
and compassion
runs so deeply.

The warrior stands firm,
the warrior stands free.
She takes on this role
to protect you,
to protect me.

For when we are lost
inside a chaotic mind,
life feels like chaos,
nothing feels fine.
We lose ourselves,
when we hear the
wrong words.
We start to believe
the pain, the hurt.

And in the haze,
the chaotic state,
the predators come
and seal our fate.
We start to slip
down the slide,
on the rollercoaster
of a chaotic mind.

The warrior shall not
walk in fear,
she shall not hide
or disappear.
She will brave
the words of pain,
she will show me how
to love again.

And just when I
begin to think,
I've turned the corner,
or reached the brink…
the love and hope
spill on the floor
and slip beneath
the lock shaped door.

And so, I go
back to work,
solving the puzzles,
unlocking the hurt.
Looking within
to one day find
what I have kept
locked deep inside
of my chaotic mind.

A Beautiful Mess

•••

Words are swirling
like a storm.
A flood of feelings
and thoughts adorn
in my mind,
safe and warm,
tucked away
so not to warn
anyone of the
mess that's there
approaching, brewing
in the air.
Words are wisdom.
Words bring hope.
Words can shield you
like a cloak.
Words inspire, and
words bring grief.
Words can rip your joy
like a thief.
Words may embrace
or shun or dull.
Words can build
empires, adventures,
and rules.
These words are stirring
up a concoction
of memories and fairytales,
of a past forgotten.
Some words are angry.
Some words are divine.

Some words are a
jumbled clutter,
but these words
are mine.
These words are my
story, and possibly
your story too.
It is imminent some
words will mean
something to you.
Words don't need to be
long or complicated;
to paint a picture,
they don't need to be
sophisticated.
My words may tremble;
my words may shake.
My words may crumble;
my words may break.
My words may rise
before they fall;
they may burn bridges
or say nothing…at all.
The words are swirling
like a storm.
It's a beautiful mess.
It's a beautiful swarm.

Missing Puzzle Peace

•••

I am a million different
puzzle pieces;
together, I am
whole.

When one goes missing,
I am broken,
searching for a piece
of my soul.

I am lost without
my pieces,
I cannot find
my peace.

I am missing the
bigger picture;
I am trying to
find me.

All of my pieces
fit together,
the picture makes
me feel alive.

When a piece—or two—
is misplaced,
I am filled with
utter strife.

I need my pieces
like I need
the rain
and shine.

I need to fill
the empty gaps
that make up
my scattered mind.

Without my pieces
fit into place
my life is a
misshapen mess.

I cannot complete
the images
that are rendering
in my head.

I want to complete
the puzzle,
my obsessions won't
let it be.

I need to see
the final picture
that belongs to
only me.

I cannot complete
the puzzle,
I cannot rest
or sleep.

I cannot feel
whole again
with these pieces
missing from me.

The puzzle is all
spread out,
it is near completed,
though

I cannot complete
the puzzle;
the misplaced masterpiece
has no home.

I need the final
product,
the art that is
my soul.

Instead, I box it
right back up,
for no one displays
a puzzle
that isn't
whole.

The Beast

•••

A thousand little pin pricks,
a thousand jabs with knives;
the pain feels easier than
the torment inside.

The darkness creeped in
while my guard was down.
I don't want to fall in…again,
I don't want to drown.

I wish I could explain it,
maybe then I could be set free
from all the angst and anger
buried inside of me.

It is a Beast, I say,
the worst kind—with fangs.
The Beast's claws are out,
it's coming for me, and
I can't go through this again.

I can't talk to just anyone,
they won't all understand.
They'll say, "Think happy thoughts instead,"
or, "This too shall pass."

The Beast does not discriminate,
it creeps up as it pleases.
Happiness is always fleeting
when the Beast needs its feeding.

Take deep breaths,
count to ten,
close your eyes,
repeat again.

Write down your thoughts,
walk in the sun,
take care of yourself,
for the Beast is not done.

The Beast can be beaten,
that's what fairytales teach us.
The Beast can be befriended,
for the Beast is within us.

Who's There?
•••

Knock knock
Who's there?
It is I,
your faithful demon;
I have come to
haunt your dreams
and slow your pace.

Knock knock
Who's there?
It is I,
your worry and doubt;
I have come to
help you second-guess
and remove yourself
from this race.

Knock knock
Who's there?
It is I,
your self-pity;
I have come to
make you writhe
and remind you of
the absence of
your worth.

Knock knock
Who's there?
It is I,
your pride;
I have come to
prevent you from
listening to others;
their experience isn't
enough.

Knock knock
Who's there?
It is I, your shame
and your regrets;
I am here,
suffocating you,
to ensure you never
forget.

The Absence of Light

•••

The darkness is my happy place,
the quiet, my solitude.
The stillness in the shadows
brings forth my fortitude.
I can keep close my demons,
I can stop pretending all is well.
I can lay my guard down;
I can place my smiles upon a shelf.
The darkness is not my enemy;
we have learned to dance quite well.
The darkness opens up my eyes
to other stories I could tell.
The absence of light is beautiful,
reminiscent, and calming too.
There is an abundance of reflection
in the dark, of things done and yet to do.
I'm grateful when the lights go out
and that stretch of darkness is near,
for I am Me inside the dark;
it is not the dark I fear.

Insomnia's Desire

•••

Sleepless nights,
restless limbs,
my mind is full
of thoughts again.

My mind races on
at lightning speeds,
thinking of possibilities,
fears, and needs.

Shut it down;
this shit's on fire.
I can't take another night
of insomnia's desire.

I made my choices,
the day is done.
My thoughts possess me;
this isn't fun.

Smoke a bit,
take a pill,
shut out night's lights,
lie calm and still.

But what about that
thing I did
years ago, when I was
just a kid?

What about that
mistake I made,
that thought I had,
those words not said?

I've now written an entire
story inside my head,
while I was lying
here in my bed.

Fuck this shit!
I need my sleep.
Insomnia's looming
without a peep.

I'm just lying here
with thoughts transpired
while hanging out
with insomnia's desire.

Redecorating

•••

Filled with ashes and embers
of the flames that slowly died,
sifting through my fingers
settling like fog over my pride.
Remaining in the shadows
as I try my best to hide;
filling this hole you left in me,
running out of time.
Stepping over the cracks
in the ocean's floor,
trying to catch my breath,
gasping for one ounce more
of the love that I once felt
now seeping under the door,
staining the rugs,
staining the walls
of the life that we adorned.

Down the Rabbit Hole

•••

Here we go down the rabbit hole
my mind is stuck in again.
At least in Alice's story
she had adventures, animals, friends.

But here inside my rabbit hole,
my mind is an endless pit.
My head is filled with words
and memories I'd rather forget.

There is no fuzzy rabbit
or potion to make me grow.
There is no smiling cat
or a table set for tea.

There's only this endless puzzle
of what happened, what-ifs,
what could be.

My head is filled with sadness.
My mind wants to break free.
But here I go, down the rabbit hole
of the trauma and heartache
that made me.

All the things that ever happened,
all the things that will never be,
tucked inside the rabbit hole,
sitting and waiting for me.

My mind is awfully tired;
my heart needs a restful sleep,
but as I shut my eyes,
my thoughts arise,
and the rabbit hole
is calling to me.

I remember the worst moments,
and I recall some happy times,
then I fall further down the
rabbit hole and consider
every
possible
outcome
that was never actually mine.

I stir up feelings
inside my head—
the best, the worst,
the eternal dread.

When do I wake up
beside the tree
and realize it was all
just a dream?

The Creature

•••

It is the habit of a creature
to run from those things it fears.
It is the habit of a creature
to fight off those things it loathes.
It is the habit of a creature
to stay near those things it understands…
and away from those it lacks.
It is the habit of a creature
to forget other creatures' pain.
It is the habit of a creature
to turn away from those in need.
It is the habit of a creature
to flee from its mistakes.
It is the habit of a creature
to live in misery,
to never love thy neighbors,
to never live free.
It is the habit of a creature
to go to sleep at night
never knowing other creatures
who choose to see the light.

Scars

•••

We all have scars we try to hide,
trauma and fear we want to disguise.
We think we're broken,
we think we aren't whole.
We think we need to
fix our soul.
We laugh at jokes that hurt our core.
We laugh and smile when we aren't sure.
We say, "I'm sorry" way too much.
We don't say, "I love you" nearly enough.
We try to cover up the pain,
we try to bury the past.
We say we're "fine"
as we put on our mask.
We hide our scars so we can blend in.
We are taught to suffer in silence.
We look for others to make us happy;
none of us know how to do this.
We think we have to be perfect
to find our perfect match.
We are so damn afraid of messing up,
we just expect that it won't last.
We choose the version to show each person;
we hide our scars and flaws.
Still, they leave, and we wonder,
did they even know me…at all?

The Weight of a Heavy Soul

•••

My soul is so heavy
as I carry it around,
the burdens of everyone
dragging me down.
The weight of the chaos
is too much to bear,
it's ripping me apart,
doing damage
without a care.
My soul is leaking,
it is punctured and torn;
it should weigh less now,
not stab me
like a thorn.
Every single worry,
every bit of pain
is adding up,
it's latching on,
I can't break free
from the weight
my soul has gained.
The chains are hot
and heavy,
they leave bruises
in their path.

My soul is bleeding now,
the damages have been
stacked
on top of one another,
it's a never ending pile
of obstacles
and inequalities,
of hate
and fear
and woe.
I carry the weight,
I can't give in.
That's what they'd love
to see me do—
just drop it all,
just say, "I can't",
just give up,
just lose…

My soul is always heavy,
for the work is never done
when you hold all the weight
of all those affected
by the evil ways of the world.

Wire Hangers and Tears

●●●

I stretched out my wire hanger
because they said I can't
control my own body
and make choices for myself.

I called a friend I trusted
I told her I needed a hand
because the politicians
and Christians
don't seem to understand.

When you try to prevent the "killing"
you leave more bodies in your path
because women will *always* decide
what kind of life we live.

So I called a friend I trusted
I asked her to come quick
because time is of the essence
when your head is on a stick.

They'll burn me at the stake
if I even survive,
they'll say I'm a murderer
but they care nothing about
my life.

So I stretched my wire hanger
and I found a safe place that would do,
I called a friend I trusted,
and she said "I've been here too".

I laid back with tears in my eyes
but not because of the potential life inside,
my tears were for me
whom no one ever hears,
they haven't cared for *my* life
even once all these years.

And if this fetus grew
and actually breathed a breath
they wouldn't care for that life either,
as pro-life
actually
means death.

So I handed my friend the hanger
and I closed my eyes in grief,
as my body is only viewed
as a baby-making machine.

I wish for more, for me, for her,
I wish for more for us
but until I have control
I'll bleed out here
in the dirt.

Tell my mom I love her,
tell everyone I fought,
tell the pro-lifers mine is over
because they prefer control.

Tell the little girls their lives
matter so much more
than this coat hanger abortion
I'm experiencing on this floor.

Then fight for them, fight for us—
every living, breathing woman
who takes her last breath—so
they can feel powerful.

Dear friend, take this hanger
and honor my choice,
don't judge me while you do,
for my life had meaning before
I was forced
to do something I never
wanted to do.

Tell the women who die in childbirth
their lives mattered too,
they should have been given the choice
to save their own lives too.

So, "godly" Christians, if you read this,
I only wish one day
that your daughters, sisters,
and mothers
are not forced into your ways.

My friend says it's time
as I look away,
as I bleed out
and cry in pain…
I wonder is this fair?
As a living, breathing woman,
is *my* life not worth their
prayers?

Suffer in Silence

•••

Let me cover these scars
before I step outside
so no one sees me
broken tonight.

Let me look at my feet
as I walk in the dark
so no one sees the
tears on my heart.

Let me patch up the cuts
and bandage the pain.
Let me pretend a while
and hold it all in.

Let me pass the places
we used to go
and forget that you don't
want me anymore.

Let me paint
my clothes in red
so no one sees the blood
my heart shed.

Let me sneak
back inside
so I can weep out
all the hurt I hide.

Let me
let you go,
or at least feel numb
until I am no more.

Little Girl Inside

•••

I want to hug the
little girl inside
who thought I'd be
loved by now.

She had a dream,
a little house by a stream,
and a partner holding
her hand.

I want to hug the
little girl inside
who had big hopes
for me.

She saw laughter
and happy ever after,
and I've let her down
again.

I want to hug the
little girl inside
who saw the
fifty years.

She saw forever,
growing old together,
she just didn't
see me.

I want to hug the
little girl inside
who had her direction
mapped out.

She had a plan,
and then I began
to grow into somebody
else.

I want to hug the
little girl inside
who thought she had plenty
of time.

She was so young,
she saw so much love,
then discovered it's not
given so freely.

I want to hug the
little girl inside
who thought it would all
work out.

She says there's a reason
for everything that happens,
but she didn't see the world
so clearly.

I want to hug the
little girl inside
and tell her
I'll be fine.

She sees me crying
and she hears me lying
to myself
on sleepless nights.

I want to hug the
little girl inside
who thought monsters were
under the bed.

She never imagined
there were actual dragons
and villains who claim
to love you.

So I'll tuck the
little girl inside
and keep her safe from
my demons.

I don't want her to see
that life isn't make-believe,
and love doesn't have
a fairytale ending.

An Ode to Art and Scars
•••

My sorrow
   and suffering
   etched on my skin.

Where does
   art stop
   and anger
   begin?

Each stabbing
   a story,
   some fun,
   some pain.

A memory
   of loss
   and heartbreak
   I gained.

We say,
   it's art,
But we all
   know,

When we choose
   our colors
   and etch
   the design,

It is
   the numbness
   we seek
   while we hide.

Behind the
   bright colors,
   the black,
   and the white

Behind the
   stab wounds
   that heal
   while we cry

We crave it
   again,
We book that
   next time

When we can
   just bleed there
   while a piece of us
   dies.

Our skin
   now beautiful
   we walk out
   with pride.

But we know
   more pain
   will draw
   on our lies.

So we find
   a new spot,
   a place
   on our skin

Where we can
   feel
   something
   again.

Unbalanced

•••

Up and down,
it's a slippery slope.
Healing, growing,
trying to cope.

My seesaw mind,
my misplaced path,
this labyrinth of emotions
I cannot mask

is eating away
at my health,
bringing me down,
I'm starting to melt.

I'm losing control,
I'm losing my grip,
feeling unbalanced,
I'm starting to slip.

Looking for security,
something to grasp.
The weight of it all—
how long will it last?

My mind is like quicksand,
pulling me down,
my feet are unsteady,
I'm starting to drown.

It's all suffocating,
these doubts and these fears,
in my unbalanced heart,
crying unbalanced tears.

I want to pick myself up
off this unbalanced floor.
I want to be better,
I want so much more

than this unbalanced life
led by my unbalanced mind.
But somewhere on my path,
I left my congruity behind.

Now I am wavering,
my footing unsteady,
while I try to get back
to a place of clarity.

An Aching Soul

•••

Strip me bare.
Peel the layers from my soul
until nothing is left
except all the love I hold.

Strip away the worry.
Strip away the pain.
Strip away the insecurity.
Leave me whole again.

I've carried it all,
all the burdens of life.
I've carried the loss,
I've carried the strife.

I sing to my demons.
I dance with my anger.
I bathe with my sorrow.
I let the past linger.

I want to break free,
I want to be new,
to wash away the bitterness,
to let the love through.

It is always there
buried deep inside,
in moments of chaos
it seems to duck and hide.

I've given my all
when there's nothing left
to give.
I've asked for nothing,
and the emptiness still
lives.

Start with the shell,
the rough, rigid surface;
crack it open;
I know I don't deserve this.

I'm tucked away in there,
I need to break out.
I'm not sure how much more
I can carry around.

Then chip away some more,
you have a ways to go.
Each layer is withered,
but it has really taken hold
and latched itself on
to my aching soul,
so do as you must,
just help me let go.

Hiding

•••

We fall into our tik toks
and book of faces,
watching everyone else
going places.
We envy,
we boast,
we wish, and
we brag,
and still we wonder
why we're sad.
We buy it all;
it's not enough,
so we buy a little more.
We want to be
like everyone else.
We forget, less is more.
We idolize people
we shouldn't.
The worthy are
left in the dust.
Sure, we give too,
but taking is a must.
We react with our thumbs,
we lead with our desires.
We all play the games,
we all follow the liars.

We want to be happy.
We want all the "likes".
Is anyone out there
really showing
who they are inside?
We hide our darkest thoughts,
we hide our inner demons.
We wait until the light
goes out,
the screen goes off,
so no one can see us.
Then the realest thoughts
creep in,
and we allow them to
keep us up.
For that is the only time of
day
when we can finally be us.

Stolen Peace

•••

And through the fog
and on top of the glass
bare feet
digging in
like a shattered past

A flicker of light
reaching out in the dark
the mind is blinded
by the heart

Picking up ashes
slide through your fingers
salty tears transform
and the pain still lingers

Stolen dances
on empty walls
fighting through the
blood stained halls

Pick a door
choose your fate
stab you
in the heart
with hate

Judgement served
conviction noted
locked away, my soul
was stolen

Sleepless Nights

•••

It was Taylor who
recognized
and identified
the tortured poets
like herself…
But there are many
of us out there
pouring our soul
through ink
onto paper
or through text
on a phone,
attempting to explain
all the words
and images
and what-ifs
and what-could-have-beens
that fill our
sleepless nights.
The rabbit holes
we run through
without looking back,
down,
down,
down
the winding spiral
of hope.

Our nights are tortured,
our minds never stop.
It is a society—or
department—
we never signed up for.
But the poet writes.
The poet aches.
The poet absolutely
breaks.
And through this torture
we create
we feel
we heal.

The Woman in the Mirror

•••

That person in the mirror
is not who she's supposed to be.
She has a lot of fire inside
and no way to set it free.
The mundane life is setting in,
but she's meant for so much more.
When you lose the motivation of your young self,
how do you find it again?
The woman in the mirror
has changed so much with age.
Others think they know her,
but they're still reading the previous page.
"You've changed," they'll say,
as if that's wrong;
though they've stayed the same
all along.
The woman in the mirror
is growing more each day.
Some days are sad, letting go
of things not meant to be.
But change, she must, to become
the person she's supposed to see.
The mirror shows all the flaws
and she continues to pick them apart.
Growing and changing isn't easy,
but staying the same isn't art.
The woman in the mirror
isn't where she's going…yet.
There are plans, and dreams,
and of course some regret.
The woman in the mirror
isn't yet who she's meant to be.
She's fueled by love and hope of more.
But all the mirrors in the world
can't change that she's still Me.

Caged Up
•••

You did this to her.
You caged her up.
You broke promises.
You didn't give her love.

You let her stop dancing.
You told her to sit down.
You silenced her voice.
You buried her crown.

You allowed her to listen
when they said she's not enough.
You should have told her,
and showed her, all of her worth.

You didn't listen
when she voiced her desires.
You shut her down,
you put out her fire.

You covered her beauty,
you watered her down.
You told her to stop
when she spoke "too" loud.

You didn't hear her,
or maybe you didn't care,
when she spoke her truth,
when she laid her pain bare.

You kept walking
when she said "slow down".
You stopped moving
when she said, "I'm ready now".

You hindered her movements,
you let her give up.
You allowed her to slip,
and made her believe she's not enough.

You allowed that girl
who had big dreams
to hide her desires,
and so it seems,
you lost her
quite a long time ago,
when you had the chance
to help her grow.

Now she's hidden,
tucked inside,
picking up the pieces
of a wasted life.

Because you allowed
others to guide you,
you let that little girl
inside you
get lost in the shuffle
and lose her way.
But it doesn't have to end
here, like this, today.

Open the cage.
Set her free.
She's waiting for you
to become her again.

Wounded. Not Broken.

•••

She has made a mess of things,
she has stumbled again.
She has been cut open,
staining the ground with her pain.

She has been wounded,
but not broken,
she has been left to bleed out.
She is now dizzy, reeling,
her head is filled with doubt.

She could call for help
or lie in her misery;
she could fight till tomorrow
and hope it's all a bad dream.

She could cling to a memory
and try to forget,
but the blood is dripping
and the pain is immense.

She is wounded, not broken,
she's been here before;
she has picked up more pieces
from this very same floor.

She has fought battles
she expected to lose;
she has tamed dragons,
she has put out a lit fuse.

She has been beat up,
emotionally drained;
she doesn't feel the strength
to fight again.

Then she remembers
the little girl in the past
who stalled, who stayed quiet,
who never talked back.

She then decided
this fight isn't just hers,
she may be wounded
but she's not broken
and she has faced much worse.

Clean up the blood.
Wipe off the pain.
Sop up the tears.
Sharpen the blade.

She takes one last look
at the mess she has made;
after this night,
she won't be the same.

Wounded.
Not broken.
She is fire.
Her wounds have spoken.

Her Body is Not Her Body

•••

Men don't deserve us.

They see us grow
human life
nourishing the
innocent,
growing little boys
big and strong.

You weak little thing,
their minds go there.

Boobs and ass.
A crevice between
our legs
where they use us
to feel safe.

You inferior being,
their minds go there.

We let them cry
in that safe space
on our chest,
while they mock us
after leaving us
on the floor.

Unworthy of our time,
their minds go there.

Their wrath fueled
when our bodies are changed,
transformed into a map
of our existence
crinkled up,
no way to smooth.

Only good for one thing,
their minds go there.

Mangled and left
on the side of the road,
a body that was never mine.
I nurtured it, loved it,
tried to keep it safe.

Piece of trash,
their minds go there.

Stripped bare
of worth
after being yearned for,
left to bleed
into the ground.

Just another whore,
their minds go there.

I clothed it.
I made it into art.
I kept it warm,
a body that was never mine.

I fought for it,
not begging a soul
to love it along with me.
I *trusted* them
with her.

Your body, my choice,
their minds go there.

I have tried to tame
the fire within her;
water her every day,
put sunshine on her face.

She.is.rage.

A crazed animal,
their minds go there.

Etched on her skin
all the joy, and pain
she has lived.

I bet she's fun in bed,
their minds go there.

Though she might
falter
she will not break,
her body is not made
of glass
but of gold
and that is why it is
being sold
at a bargain
at the auction
as they yell
out her value.

Her body is not her own.

It is okay to cry.

Awakening in the Storm.

They Took it From Me

•••

So many things I have loved,
they took those from me.

Sitting in solitude
and silence
under the stars.

Taking a walk in the
sunshine,
or by the light of the moon.

Enjoying a meal,
solo
in peace.

Listening to music
that soothes my soul
while resting
under a tree.

Reading a book
in a local café,
enjoying the scenery
and buzz of the people.

They took it from me.

They have me choosing
encounters with bears
over encounters
with men.

Giggling with girlfriends
over dinner, or a drink.
They invited themselves
into our party.

And they took it from me.

They started this war.

All *we* asked for was peace.

I Fell Apart

•••

I fell apart
from each broken
heart

and all that pain
made me feel shame

I didn't know
where I would go
how I would heal
how true love feels…

I let the boys
use me like a toy
they called it love
and I didn't know much
about how love worked

and so I believed
that's how love's supposed
to be…
so I let them
break me

all of those times
I didn't realize
I held the power
that I was stronger

so, now, I'm taking it back…

all of these scars
are beautiful marks
of who I've become
since I learned to love
who I am now
and who I used to be
all of the
versions
of me

the misshaped scars
the broken parts
the bandaged and bruised
all of my wounds

they are the map
to my painful past
and also the path
to meet me where I'm at…

so don't come around
thinking
you'll break me down

that girl who I was
who used to get shoved

well, now she's tough
and she's had enough
and no one is holding her
down

Burning the Witches

•••

They tried to burn us—
the women, not witches.
Then they try to control us
and when we speak up
we're called bitches.

They think that we owe them
our time and attention,
simply because they interrupt us
when we're out on our missions.

They gawk at us as we walk by,
waiting for their time to strike.
They may say, "Hey sexy" or
"You should smile, sweetie";
and they expect us to respond
even though we didn't ask
to be greeted.

We are called hateful,
bitchy, and rude
just because we don't want
to be bothered by dudes.

We try so hard to go about
our business,
running our errands,
climbing ladders, or fitness.
But as soon as *one* guy
decides to approach,
we are expected to stop
our lives and swoon
while he boasts.

And saying no is ever enough,
they can't be *embarrassed*,
they have to act tough,
and puff out their chests,
stand taller and proud,
just because a woman
turned them down.

So again, we're harassed,
ridiculed, assaulted, or stalked,
simply because we wanted
to go for a walk.

And still they wonder
why we're so angry,
why we're on edge,
why we walk hastily…

Because we know they burn
women, not witches.
Because melting us down
has always been their intention.

Speak Up!

•••

Don't turn a blind eye
to the hate that you see…
speak.
Don't laugh at their setbacks
they are trying to break…
speak.
Don't say "not all men";
it's never enough.
Speak up!
When you view cruelty,
racism, and hostility,
use your privilege, acceptance,
or just your ability,
and speak up!
History shows us
these problems aren't new.
It's easy to ignore when
the target isn't you.
Don't trust that someone else
will step up…
speak up!
When you witness terror,
violence, or animosity,
hold your head up…
and speak up!
You say, "I'm not racist,"
but is that enough?
Speak up!
We can fight white supremacy,
violence against women,
and such stuff…
if we all, each one of us,
simply speaks up.

Such Pitiful Things

•••

Women have forever been the nurturers, the care takers, the lifters of hearts…even those who have never given birth.

Women have been the vessels of souls.

Yet, all across the globe we see women treated as less than, inferior, controlled, objects for a man's use; such pitiful things.

Women are targeted, preyed upon, belittled, tortured.

And who picks up the pieces and attends to women after being violated by man?

Other women.

Women are more powerful together. So why, beautiful ladies, girls, and women, why do we not lift each other more?

We only have each other.

Ally

•••

I have so many things to say,
but I don't want to take
your voice away.
Your experience and truth
deserve recognition;
I am here on your side,
but is it my place to mention?
The empath in me
wants to scream loud,
but it is your reality
we are talking about.
I want to be a friend, an ally,
but how?

Am I saying enough?
Am I saying too much?
I want to understand;
I want to speak up.

It is not my intention
to drown out your words;
I just want to support each of
you,
I want *you* to be heard

Yes, I will listen;
I want to know more.
I don't want to be just
another *white girl*
who is drawing attention
away from your truth,
away from your anger,
your pain…
away from your roots.

This world we live in
has always existed.
There have always been allies

right there, resisting.
I don't want to be
in the front of the pack.
I just want to show others
how to have every human's
back.

My heart shatters
every damn time
another life is taken…stolen,
no longer to shine.
But this isn't *my* reality,
it isn't *my* life.
My white skin
gives me privilege;
it buys me more time.

My words should never
matter more than yours,
but if I can change just one
mind,
to show others your worth,
then I have to try;
I have to say more.
But I'm always ready
to shut up and listen,
to help find a cure.

I have zero answers,
I am just fueled with love
for every human facing
adversity—
everyone who's been shoved.

Some say too much,
some never enough.
All I have are my words.
All I have is my love.

Tone it Down

•••

Too much passion?
What is that?
Can one care too much?

Take off that crown
that you found;
you need to tone it down.

The cat-callers are out.
Don't make a scene.
Surely, you can walk on by.

When you're told to smile,
not frown,
don't shout or scream,
please, just tone it down.

You're angry because
he grabbed your arm;
he just wanted your attention.

There is no need
to fuss about.
Quiet. Tone it down.

These strangers are beginning
to stare at us;
it's causing me much grief.
I know you are standing up
for yourself—
that is your belief.

In this life, this is just
the way things are.
Your intensity is way too
much now.
Please, just tone it down.

I'll say this much…
my anger is not enough,
and I won't be intimidated…
by a heckler, a harasser,
an abuser, or a bully.
I'll shut them down,
I'll call them out;
I will stand my ground.
No matter who looks,
no matter who sees,
I will not tone it down.

BLFM

•••

When white owns up to hate of the past
and the present...
when police are held accountable
and stop murdering on the street,
that is when we will be
on our way to peace.

When we can *all* walk into a store
on a cold day
with our hoodies on
and not be eyed down like thieves,
that is when we will be
on our way to peace.

When *every* parent has the *same* fears
as their child grows and learns who to be,
that is when we will be
on our way to peace.

When every Black man and woman
no longer holds their breath
when those reds and blues start flashing
and they are pulled from their seat,
that is when we will be
on our way to peace.

When justice is no longer an answer
of finally...*finally*,
but of the norm and regularity,
that is when we will be
on our way to peace.

When our Black brothers and sisters
are no longer burying their children
because of skin color, hate,
or ideas of supremacy,
that is when we will be
on our way to peace.

When we all stand up and say
enough is enough,
when we finally stop allowing
white men to act tough,
when we stop being cowards
and show Black people love,
that is when we will be
on our way to peace.

When we replace the crowns
that were stolen,
and honor their skin, their hair,
their culture…
when we decide *true* justice
should come before, not after, because
Black lives fucking matter.

Tiny Minds

•••

A tiny town
with tiny minds,
flashing their hate,
showing the signs
that evil is rooted
inside their religion,
not accepting others
who aren't *just* like them.

I didn't belong.
I didn't fit in.
So I took my tiny mind
from that tiny town
searching for a place
to begin again.

I brought my tiny mind
from my tiny town
and immersed it in views
I had never been around.

I shut up.
I listened.
I heard.
I learned.

My tiny mind learned
what it's like to love
others who are different,
to stand up for those
who've been shoved.

I tripped and I fell;
I remember weak moments.
I thought I was superior,
that my self-pride was
being stolen.

"Why can't I celebrate
this white skin I'm in?"

Oh, child, please sit down,
let's try this again.

My twenties were full
of lessons, hard truths.
Sure, I had fun,
but at what expense
to you?

But at some point, we get to
decide, to choose…
do we keep our tiny minds
in our tiny towns
till we're through?

Or do we read more,
and listen to those
who have lived different lives,
who have walked different
roads?

Can you shut up
for just a few minutes?
Can you expand your tiny
mind;
can you please listen?

When others speak their truth
about the life *they* live,
stop trying to make yours
sound worse,
like you've been in their
shoes.

When they say that their
people
are being gunned down,
that they lost another friend—
a brother, a sister, a town,

64

it's because they are living
this truth
every day;
they can't even walk into
your tiny store with grace.

Because if they do,
they look awful suspicious.
You follow them with your
eyes;
you expect that they're
vicious.

You allow your children
to see you too;
you teach them these things,
you shrink *their* minds too.

It is simply not hard
to pick up a book,
to expand your tiny mind,
to change how you look
at others not like you,
who have different roots,
who have different beliefs,
who have different truths.

Tiny towns can be great
for family and safety,
until you are *different*
and the tiny minds don't trust
you.

If you're just another tiny
mind
from a tiny town,
do yourself a favor…
venture out.

Listen, and then, just maybe
you can understand how
other tiny minds are growing.

And if you refuse…
well, your white privilege
is showing.

Audacity

●●●

Our shorts are too short,
our shorts are too long;
we get judged in long dresses
and judged in a thong.

You say our eyelashes are too long,
our makeup too thick,
then we watch you gawk over models
and I am just so damn sick
of fighting this battle;
our bodies aren't sexual objects
for which you can just pick
and choose who is worthy
and choose who is beauty
and choose who you respect.

As soon as we say,
"Don't do that; we don't like it".
It's "Yeah right" or "Come on baby"
"It's just a joke; don't try to fight it".

We can't be topless for comfort—
either society says not to
or men gawk
and make us not want to.

We can't talk about our own bodies
without your disgust or sexual desire
lingering there, ready to ignite
like fire.

We can't just be human;
we have to be "sexy" or "pretty".
If we want to be friends,
you make up a "zone" that you fit in.

We can't just be kind,
for we *must* be flirting;
to smile at you…like that…
you think we are yearning
to have you touch us,

and so you do, without consent
because goddess forbid
we just want to be friends.

You place your hands
on the smalls of our backs
just to pass by
with all the respect that you lack.

Please tell me the last time
you put your hands
on the low back
of another man
just to say "excuse me"
like words just won't do;
you think we want to feel
those dirty fingers from you?

You think you have permission
to say what you please,
to call us "sexy" or "baby",
like we don't have our own names.

You say we're "uptight" or "stuck up"
when we say, just speak to us like humans—
like you actually have a brain!

We don't owe you a thing
just because you buy dinner.
We don't have to speak to you
just because you sent a message.

We owe you *nothing*—
not our words or our bodies.
And you think we "can't take a compliment"
when you call us a "hottie".

You actually believe
you're entitled to us…
oh, you're just "being nice"
until you call us *sluts*
because we decline
your not-so-subtle passes,
so you run back to the locker room

to talk about our asses.

You actually believe
this is normal behavior.
You actually believe
we are "men-haters"
simply because we
are fucking fed up
with all of your bullshit,
and it's just so fucked up
that you can't even glimpse
all the shit we go through,
all the slut-shaming posts,
all the body shaming too.

You rate us with numbers,
you undress us with your eyes,
and you still wonder
why we are so sick of guys?

You do yourself no favors
by continuing on,
but oh, of course, you have something
to say when we're done.

You don't listen to all the others
who are saying the same thing,
that *every* woman has suffered
from your misogynistic games.

Your mother, your sisters,
your daughters, your aunts…
every last one of us
have danced this dance.

We've had to put on
the fakest of smiles,
we've had to fake kindness—
and weakness—
just so we could put miles
in between some man and me…
just to make men leave us be.

We've had to allow men to kiss us
whether we wanted to or not,
and allow hugs to linger,
so we don't get him so hot
that his temper boils over—
then we aren't safe.

We have to look forward and backward
in every damn place
that we go
that we walk
sometimes grabbing a stranger
to fake a talk
just to slip away
from the men who linger and stare
a little too long,
and if we dare
go out alone
or wear short dresses,
it's *our* fault
and we have to clean up *your* messes.

Then we are crucified
for making tough decisions,
for making choices
we never wanted to be in.

Do we just look the other way
and hope the strange man goes away?

Or do we make our voices loud
and hope we draw in a crowd,
so these men will leave us be?
We're never right; you won't let us be.

We don't "hate men",
we hate the type
who can't even see
what women fight
against each day—
and for centuries now.

We just want it to stop.
Yet, still we won't bow
to your audacity
to your toxic ways.
We will just get up and fight
another damn day.

Silly Woman

●●●

Stand up straight,
smile pretty now.
Speak gently and softly;
don't cause a scene.
Nod in agreement,
be cordial and kind.
Don't speak up, lady,
just fall in line.

Mind your manner,
follow the men.
Raise the children,
and to the home
you'll tend.

Don't use profanity,
it's not lady-like.
Learn when to listen,
only respond in polite.

Pay a little extra
for good hygiene.
Buy the lady razors—
and all things pink.

Shave your legs and arms
before the men see.
Dress up really nice,
be sure to act girly.

Wear something feminine,
but not too sexy,
for you are at fault if
the men cannot control
their urges.

Don't walk alone
or go out at night,
for the men have only
one thing on their minds.

Don't have too much sex,
but don't be a prude.
Say something sweet
when a man is speaking
to you.

Walk around with a constant
smile on your face,
for there is nothing worse than
a woman who just wants
to think.

Teach your daughters how
to be a good girl,
that no matter what happens
it's just the way of the world.

There is no sense in standing
up for yourself
or standing up to a man.
The world just won't believe
you
and you'll be reprimanded
while he gets a slap
on the hand.

Just do as you're told
and all will be fine.
Keep your head down;
walk a straight line.

Be forever grateful
when you find a man
to keep you;
you certainly don't want to
know
what single women
go through.

Tell your boys to try again
whenever a girl tells them
"No",
because we all know "no"
means "maybe"—
that's just how love goes.

If you weren't so pretty
boys wouldn't be so keen
to get in your panties,
to take what they need.

But if you dress down,
you won't be taken seriously,
so just be thankful
that men even want you.

Wake up early,
make up your face,
start breakfast for him,
after all, that's your place.

If he wants a child,
you'll carry it till due.
Oh, you aren't ready yet?
Well, it isn't up to you.

Your body isn't yours
to do as you please.
You silly woman,
don't you see?

It's just not sexy to be
confident
or strong,
to make your own choices,
to not know where you
belong.

"All men are created equal"
does not include you.
Oh, you silly woman,
life isn't up to you.

You're meant to believe
that men control all,
that you are inferior,
your mind is small.

You could never make it
out on your own;
be thankful the man
gave you a house—a home.

Be thankful he didn't
hit your face
and hid the bruises
in another place.

You still have to answer
for the things you have done,
for not doing as told,
for not staying home.

Pick up the mess
because it's all your fault;
if you had just listened,
he wouldn't be so hot.

The man is sorry;
you must forgive,
for nothing matters more
than a complete family
for the kids.

If you walk away
and try to start again,
you *will* be judged
by other men and friends.

You silly woman,
when will you learn;
if you talk back or speak up,
you'll get what you deserve.

It's just like the '50s,
though it's 2025.
You don't get a choice
because they are pro-life.

Let the man place his hands
wherever we wants;
he's just being kind.
After all, you did flaunt
by wearing that skirt,
and painting your lips,
and walking with that
sway in your hips.

You curled your hair
and colored your eyes,
so you *must* be trying
to tempt these guys.

You drank too much,
you fell asleep;
you should have more
self-control and blame
yourself
for the company you keep.

You don't want kids?
What's wrong with you?
You'll never have meaning
without a child…or two.

Oh, silly woman,
you'll change your mind,
and you'll know when
the time is right…
to put aside your selfish ways
and just do as male society
says.

Don't call yourself a feminist—
it means you hate men!
How could you ever think
something is wrong with
them?

They've had the power
so very long,
that's just the way it is.
Women trying to have a say—
what kind of shit is this?

Oh, silly woman,
don't wait too long
to find a beau;
the older and more
single you are,
they'll surely say
you're a "ho".

Oh, silly woman,
straighten your crown,
this is a story of chauvinistic
men.
Surely you know it's not the
end
until women run the world.

Gone are the Days

•••

Because I'm a feminist
you call me a "man-hater",
because I call out your toxicity,
because I call out your anger.
The anger you have
for losing control,
because women aren't dealing
with your bullshit anymore.

You seem awfully pissed
because we "can't take a joke",
although you think it's funny
to laugh at our bodies—to feel in control.
And then we make you feel
insignificant and small
when we call you out,
when we stand tall.

So you hurl a few more insults,
because you're "such a man".
So the cycle continues
just as it began.
As long as there is at least
one "bro" who thinks you're funny,
you will keep bashing women,
you will keep saying *something*.
You really don't realize
we have been preparing for this
our entire lives,
since we were kids.
We have heard it all
from men before—
the crude jokes,
snide remarks,
glaring eyes…

anything you can do to
make us feel small inside.

And when we say
"enough is enough",
and we speak out,
and we get tough,
you think we "hate men".
Well, why do you think?
Is it because you actually *do* know
that most men are creeps?
You've seen it too,
of course you have.
That "locker room talk"
actually *is* really bad.
You chalk it up to
"guys being guys",
but maybe what you
don't realize
is that your "bros"
are *actually* capable
of acting on their thoughts,
yet *you* won't hold them
accountable.

So you just laugh
when they "joke" about
"banging that drunk chick"
and you say something equally creepy
like, "I wish I could hit that".
Because your reality
is nothing like ours;
you've been allowed to be
creepy, gross, and foul,
while we were expected
to just allow
your awful behavior,
to swallow our words,
to "act like a lady",
to never be heard.
We are literally conditioned
for this from birth.

So now that we've taken
all that we can,
now that we've heard it
over and over again,

now that we're tired,
exhausted, and spent
from being torn down
from hearing your "hints"…
as soon as we say no more,
not one more day,
will we accept your world,
will we stay in "our place".

The very moment we stand up
for ourselves
we get called "man-haters"
because we refuse to bow
to your continued "bro jokes",
to your toxic masculinity,
because we refuse to continue
this expected complacency.
Then you come at us with that
"not all men" shit,
like we don't know
there *are* good men.
But if you were one of them
you wouldn't be so triggered
when I call men out,
when I make myself bigger—
bigger than all of your misogynistic
jokes—
when I speak my truth,
when I call out your "bros".
If the jokes you find funny
are about women's bodies,
then I feel sorry for your sisters,
your daughters, your mamas.
It sounds like you're mad
that women no longer need you,
that you actually have to *try*
to get someone who even *wants* you.
Gone are the days
when "boys will be boys".
We don't play that shit here;
we're here to make noise.

Straighten Your Crown

•••

Wake up.
Get busy.
Tear it down.
When you are done,
straighten your crown.

Show up.
Speak up.
Say it out loud.
And don't forget to
straighten your crown.

Step up.
Fight hard.
Don't back down.
It may slip, so be sure to
straighten your crown.

Take a breather
when the fight is tough.
Be sure to rest, sit down.
Then rise up ready,
join us again
as you straighten your crown.

The women before us
fought hard, fought loud.
We won't stop until we
make them proud.

Link arms.
Hold hands.
The time is now
to help your sisters
straighten their crowns.

In My Womb

•••

In my womb
there is no room
for your opinions,
religion, or laws.

In my womb
there is no room
for a child
you will never protect.

In my womb
there is no room
for a fetus
I never asked for.

In my womb
there is no room
for your politics
or views on gender.

In my womb
I choose whom
will reside or
whom I will reject.

In my womb
there is no room
for your bounty
on my head.

In my womb
there is no room
for any man's
opinion.

You pump three times,
your sperm is now mine,
so I will choose what
to do with it.

In my womb
I will choose
how my body is
used.

My womb is mine
and I don't have time
for your ideas on how
I should manage it.

The Existence of Woman

•••

Ladies,
You do not have to be nice.
We were not put on this planet
to be nice.
We don't have to "respect our elders"
simply due to age.
We don't have to "respect a uniform"
or a badge.
We don't have to move out of their way
when they choose to walk directly
in our path.
We don't have to smile
simply because we are in their presence.
We are the essence
of all life.
We shall walk with grace
and confidence.
We shall take our place
in all spaces where we exist.
We do not have to ask for permission
to exist.
We do not have to agree
because a man says it is so.
And we are allowed
to say no.
We will not go quietly
into the night,
but stand strong
within the light.
We will choose the tiger,
the lion,
the bear
until man can be trusted
to keep us safe.
We shall build community
amongst each other
and help others
whenever we can.

We shall hold onto
that spark that makes us
human,
that makes us
women.
We shall not bow down,
as we are not inferior beings.
We shall live as we wish.
simply because we exist;
breathe our air
as we see fit.

Declining Your Hate

•••

Take your words
and your bitterness.
Take your judgements,
I'm through with this.
Take your hate
and your twisted ego.
Take your stupidity;
I'm not stooping that low.
Take your racism
and your abhorrent views.
Take your backwards
thinking,
I'm done with you.
There is no space
for your kind here.
We are too busy
cleaning out the fear.
We don't have time
for your toxicity and games.
We don't have energy
for your corrupt ways.
We do not accept
your hate, your loathing,
as you sit over there
doing absolutely nothing
to make this world better,
to make yourself great.
We don't give a shit
what you think.

So take your ugly stares
and venomous glances;
we'll still be here
laughing and dancing.
You can't fight fire with wind,
and that's all you do,
you keep blowing out air
as you yap and you stew
over all these humans
living their lives,
loving their neighbors,
and calling out guys
like you…and your crew
who have absolutely nothing
better to do.
So, take your opinions
and ball them right up;
throw them right in the trash
because we don't give a fuck.

Woman, I See You

•••

Woman, I see you.
I see your exhaustion.
Yet, you keep fighting
despite these thoughts
that you're lost in.

Woman, I see you.
I see your heartache.
Yet, you keep loving
despite the amount
your soul breaks.

Woman, I see you.
I see your anger.
Yet, you keep smiling
despite the pain
that still lingers.

Woman, I see you.
I see your grace.
I see your beauty.
I see your strength.

Woman, I see you.
I see your fight.
I see you love
with all of your might.

Woman, I see you.
You never bow down.
You never give up.
You never drown.

Woman, I see you,
stronger than you know.
You are amazing.
You are worthy.
Please keep going, and
you'll reap what you sow.

Hold On, Dear Girl

•••

Our grandmothers fought this fight
to ensure we had more rights,
only for us to watch their children take it from us.

But remember, dear girl,
women have been fighting for years,
secretly plotting, over tea,
waiting for the right moment to strike.

We are not powerless, dear girl.
We actually hold the power, tightly,
when we lock hands together.

So, hold on, dear girl, hold on.

Underground. Above ground.
In the day or in the night.
Out in the open, or hidden in secret.
Out loud. Or oh, so quiet.

Power is not in the physical strength of men and their control.
The power is in our resolve to breathe new life right into this
world.

As mothers. As aunties.
As sisters. As friends.
When we fight,
we win.

Hold on, dear girl, hold on.

It may not be the tomorrow we hoped for.
But remember, it's not the end.
They promised hate.
But love always wins.
Don't show your love to man, dear girl.
Show your love to friends.
Care for the other girls, dear girl.
Hold each other's hands.

Whether you fight in darkness or light,
whether you fight with words or swords,
remember, all the little girls you know…
their fight is in our hands.

Hold on, dear girl, hold on.

Hold on, dear girl. Hold. On.

An Empath's Fire

•••

She walked such a fine line of
passion and anger,
she forgot which she was…

Angry because she felt herself
in a glass room,
muted, her words simply bouncing
around the walls.

Everyone sees. No one listens.

She is sad when they are crying.
She hurts when they feel pain.
She feels fear when they are afraid.
Her heart breaks when they beg.

She screams.

Everyone sees. No one listens.

She watches the hate from behind
the glass.
She watches their tears fall to the floor,
her own tears forming a puddle
below her feet.

She bangs on the wall and prepares
a fire to burn it down.
She will suffer so others can prevail.
She yells out cold, harsh truths
that everyone sees, but no one listens.

She is a vessel of passion and anger.
She feels every emotion from the ones
who fall down,
the ones who are kicked,
the ones clawing the ground,
just for an ounce of dignity and respect,
just for an ounce of love.

She doesn't know how to help.
Her words are not heard.
Her pain flowing from her eyes.
Her anger starting to rise.

She will keep standing.
She will still yell.
She will scream louder.
She will raise hell.

This isn't the day
she decides to simmer down.
This isn't the time
to give up, not now.

She has faced a thousand hells
before this life, this day, this hour.
This is not the day she loses
her power.

She is not capable of giving up;
she has walked harder paths
and she continues still.

She stands proudly on that thin line
of passion and anger.
She dares them all
to show themselves.

For when their hate comes to light,
she won't go down without a fight.

Paper Castle

•••

There are
black walls
in my
paper castle

There are
slippery slopes
leading
to the door

There's a
sealed gate
you can't
come through

And I'm
the dragon
tired of
this war

There are
thin walls
around my
paper castle

It wouldn't
take much
to bring
them down

One breath
of fire, or
a few drops of water
to make them melt

There are
blood walls
in my
paper castle

Sacrifices
from the
mistakes
I've made

There are
iron bars
around
every corner

Your weapons
would make
my
day

Give me
a reason
to burn down
this place

Don't tempt
the dragon
in a
paper castle

Don't mock
her
or you'll get
burned

Don't threaten
with your demons
I promise
mine are worse

There are
sad walls
in my
paper castle

There are
no pictures
on these
walls

There are
angry voices
in my
paper castle

Don't believe
you
can make them
soft

There are
shattered dreams
in my
paper castle

You're too
late
to make them
come true

There is
so much anger
in my
paper castle

Turn around
before
the dragon
sees you

She can't
be tamed

She is
through

It is okay to scream.

enCHANTments.

Words of a Feather

•••

As I write the words I feel
the words spill out
the words, they heal
sometimes they hurt
and break apart
as they fall to the page
like splattered art
my words may bring wisdom
my words may bring peace
or they may cause heartache,
anger, or worse;
my words may be a feather,
or a dagger,
or a curse.

Healing

•••

Heart burn, yeah,
a million bruises.
Dragged through the dirt
like I'm useless.

Gut punch, yeah,
I'm still losing.
It's all dead,
throw out the roses.

Soul pain, yeah,
grave digging.
Life on repeat.
Why am I living?

Crushed hope, yeah,
over-dreaming.
It's all fucked
this air I'm breathing.

Breath lost, yeah,
summer drowning.
Cut off this shit
I'm allowing.

Fuck this, yeah,
I don't need it.
You ran while
I was bleeding.

Restless nights, yeah,
from stolen kisses.
Can't shake off
this pain I'm feeling.

Body buried, yeah,
failed mission.
Want to return
as something different.

Cloudy skies, yeah,
broken promises.
Rain in my eyes;
you know you did this.

Numb body, yeah,
don't want to feel it.
New scars appearing;
does that mean I'm healing?

The Tag of Shame

•••

I ripped it out,
that letter, that number
that tells others
my worth;
the value of the dress
a separate tag entirely,
the value of my body,
sewn tightly within it.

I may have torn
the slightest hole
to rip it from
its seams,
but I wanted it out,
I needed it gone,
before anyone could see.

It brushed too deeply
onto my skin
with every step I took,
reminding me
that sizing me
is written in
society's book.

Last year there was
a different letter,
a smaller number…
and still smaller
the year before.

Those tags remain,
because they don't
bring shame
or pain
when I throw them
on the floor.

She's got such
a pretty face,
it's her body that needs
some work.
I can't believe
she let herself go…

Will they ever learn?

And so I ripped it out,
the tag that labels
my worth.
I threw it down
onto the ground,
struck a match
and watched it burn.

7 Deadly Sins

•••

I am beauty and intelligence
and far superior to all.
I feel no need for apologies
and have no concerns with
making others feel small.

I have paved my own path
and made my own way.
I have accumulated my
wealth and success
so others can do the same.

I am anger and venom,
you must listen to me.
My fury is raging;
it is all I can see.

I yearn and I crave,
I covet and want
everything that they have,
everything that they flaunt.

I long for a touch
I know I don't need.
My fiery passion
is overwhelming;
on desire I feed.

My insatiable appetite
is taking control.
I indulge in my cravings
when the hunger unfolds.

Now I'm quite sluggish—
no motivation or spark.
I welcome the idleness,
no work shall I impart.

They say I'm a sinner,
they say I should repent.
I say I'm just human,
don't hate me,
hate the sin.

Ink

•••

I
ink
my skin
and they tell me
I'm no longer
beautiful,
a body
no longer
pure.

My ink
tells my
stories
and still
they think
they deserve
more.

Etched
on my skin
the losses
heartbreaks
adventures
and memories
that have shaped
my life
my journey
my path.

Still
they think
my stories
are for them
to know.

I carry
my stories
inked
into my skin,
my body
a walking
canvas.

I do not ask
the painter
what the painting
means.
I simply enjoy
the beauty.

Daughters of Inequality

•••

Under his eye…
the eye of man,
but we are *not*
going back there again.

You take our pay,
you take our choice,
you take our dignity,
you *won't* take our voice.

We are the daughters of women
raised on inequality.
We were told we could be
anything we wanted to be.

You are so pro-life
that you want to end *mine,*
just for another lost soul
to be in the system, in line.

You want us to smile
and let down our hair.
You think we are objects
no matter what we wear.

It is *our* fault you rape us
and we are never believed,
because we are just so emotional,
unbelievable beings.

You think we want to murder babies;
you think it's all about you.
Yet you have never stepped up to care
for a stranger's child, have you?

You think we'll just listen, and oblige,
and give up.
But you have no idea how long
this war has been waging for us.

I think you're just scared,
you've lost all control.
The white man is *so* little, now
and so disrespected…
rightfully so.

So hold on to that power
as long as you can.
We are raising young women
who will never back down.

Pass your man-laws,
do as you will,
because you're fueling the fire
on how women feel.

Just as you have always done,
we'll do as we please;
we'll do what we need.
We do *not* accept any man's
laws about our own bodies.

Do No Harm, Teach No Hate

•••

Stop teaching boys to "try harder"
when a girl tells them no.
Stop teaching girls a boy must like them
when they hit them, or tease them, just for show.
Stop worrying about what's inside a kid's pants;
"Is it a boy or a girl?"—stop asking parents
these stupid questions, as if it matters
which toilet we should use,
or who we *should* find attractive.
Pink isn't for girls,
blue isn't for boys.
They're just colors,
they're just toys.
Let your child's imagination flow;
teach them to be *happy*, not to put on a show
just because society says so.

The world has never been black or white,
humans made it this way,
humans started this fight.
Women aren't "weak" and men aren't "strong".
We all have fucking feelings; we all belong.
We all have love we want to give;
we all have fears, we all just want to live
our lives the way we see fit.

Stop boxing people up like you pack away clothes—
these for the summer, these for the snow.
We don't have to fit in any category;
we aren't fucking objects, we just want to be
free to love, free to speak
our truth, our pain, free to find our peace.

Stop worrying about what is under someone's clothes,
or who they love, or what life they chose.
Focus that attention on yourself;
maybe figure out why you have
all this anger you've always felt.

Do no harm,
teach no hate,
maybe even try to celebrate
that we are advancing,
we are breaking out of norms
that society always told us
we were *supposed* to form.
If you're not growing,
if you're just standing still,
then we don't give a shit how you feel
about our confidence,
about our progress;
I feel sorry for you,
because you just don't get it.
We will continue to hang our rainbow flags,
to shout "Black lives matter",
to support fabulous men in drag.
Your hate hasn't stopped us so far.
What makes you think we care about your feelings...at all?

Built on the Backs of Black

•••

I am fueled by anger.
Anger streams out
like tears from my eyes,
overflowing,
just one match to ignite.

Too many people have forgotten
that Black women raised
the white children
whose descendants
now dance on their graves.

Black women have been the backbone
of white progression, of white success.
Black women have lifted themselves
from the embers
of the fires
white people left behind
as they burned them to the ground.

And still, they rise.
(Thank you, Maya.)
They rise,
they dance,
they laugh,
and they love.
They live.
Despite the treacherous obstacles
placed directly, purposefully
in their path.
They stomp through the mud.
They play in the puddles.
They smile, and they sing.
They lead.
Some out loud.
And some in peace.
But still, they lead.

They have every right to imagine
burning it all down
to ash and rubble; start anew; or let it all die, completely.
Instead, they are the definition of resilience.
And we need every one of them
in this resistance.

Their very neighbors and friends
have once again
betrayed them.
They have reminded them
they don't trust them to lead.
And still, they rise.
(Thank you, Maya.)

We mourn for the small progress lost.
We mourn for the children we were, who saw hope in the future.
We mourn for the respect that slipped away…or was maybe never
earned.
We mourn for women, for Trans, for Gays.
And I mourn for Black women
who paved the way
while white society
pushed them away.

We were all built
on the very backs
of Black women,
and still,
we aren't satisfied.
Still, we demand more.
Still, we try everything
to break them.
And still, they rise.
(Thank you, Maya.)

Apologies mean nothing
without change.
Policies mean nothing
if Black women are last.

And still they try.
And still they rise.
And still they fight.

The Women Before Us

•••

We watched the women before us
crawl through the dirt
just to be viewed as capable.

The women before us
battled coat hangers
while we battle
a bounty on our heads.

We strive to teach
sex education
while you strive
for control.

The women before us
fought for bank accounts
while we fight for
equality and respect.

We have been fighting
for the same damn shit
for generations,
and yet you still can't admit
you're wrong.

You feel the need
to chime in,
"not all men";
for fuck's sake,
we know.

You call yourself a "nice guy"
but you call us "fat" or "ugly"
as soon as we reject you.

You call yourself "pro-life"
but you don't give two fucks
about mine.

We watched the women before us
put up with your shit—
your lies and control
and manipulation,
and you're losing control because
we are sick of it.

The women before us
had to secretly fight,
they bowed their heads,
they stayed quiet.
But we are not the women
of then;
we are the women who
call out men.

We do not accept
your views, your laws.
We reject your backwards ways,
we reject you making the calls.

The women before us
paved the way.
Each generation is stronger,
day after day.

The women before us
started the fight we're in;
now we tear apart
the patriarchy
limb from limb.

Sorry Not Sorry

•••

Here I go,
saying "sorry" again—
sorry I'm not enough,
sorry you can't stand
to listen to women…
to understand.

I'm sorry you don't meet
my qualifications,
I'm sorry I won't settle
for less.
I'm sorry I didn't reply
when you cat-called me;
I'm sorry I'm not always
my best.

I'm sorry you don't like it
when I do as I please.
I'm sorry I don't need you,
as you might believe.

I'm sorry my success
makes you feel insecure.
I'm sorry I get angry
when I don't feel heard.

I'm sorry for dressing
in a way that brings attention.
I'm sorry you don't receive
a hundred percent of my
affection.

I'm sorry I'm Me,
and oh, did I mention,
I'm sorry I'm *not* sorry
if you lack reprehension.

For I will never be sorry
for being who I am.
I'm done apologizing
to these pretentious men.

Catcaller Alley

•••

Wrap my hands
around his neck;
It's really sad
when they're
not dead yet.
He says my physique
isn't strong enough;
he'll think again,
dragged behind his truck.

I only wanted
to be left alone,
walking Catcaller Alley
on my way home.
Ignoring them
just won't do
when they think your body
doesn't belong to you.

Pull the knife
from my purse,
he's leaving here
in a hearse.
Taking back
what is mine;
after all, not smiling
is my only crime.

I promise I tried
to walk away,
but men see "No"
as a little game.

First, you're "sexy",
then you're a slut;
they'll never stop
or have enough.

Now I'm smiling,
oh, so sweet,
as he bleeds out at my feet.

Being polite
never works,
but now I think
I've found the cure.

Cut them up,
watch them fall.
Shut them up
once and for all.

Women Aren't a Game

•••

Women aren't a game
that boys get to play.
Women aren't chess pieces
that boys choose to move
or stay.

Women aren't toys
that boys get to throw.
Women aren't dogs
that boys get to tell "No".

Women aren't objects
that boys place on a shelf.
Women aren't souvenirs
that boys buy for themselves.

Women aren't chairs
that boys pile their shit on.
Women aren't puppets
that boys keep a tight string
on.

Women aren't items
that boys think they own.
Women aren't garbage
that boys dispose of when
done.

Women are literal
vessels of souls.
Women bring all of the boys
into this world.

Women have watched
these boys play these games,
and boys think women don't
know
the boys' deceitful ways.

Women aren't stupid,
and women aren't yours
to do with as you please,
you clueless, selfish boys.

You Don't See Me

•••

You paint an image of me
in your head
because of some post I wrote
that you read.

You picked my tone.
You picked my manner.
You decided you know me
because of social media
banter.

You warn others
I may be angry,
I may hate men…
and likely hate babies.

You have your story
you've written of me.
You've painted an image
for others to see…

But you don't see me
when I'm having
deep conversations with
friends about hard stuff.

You don't see me
when I'm laughing till I cry
with people who bring
absolute joy to my life.

You don't see me gush
over my goddess daughter
or sing silly songs
to my old chihuahua about
how handsome he is.
You don't see me
when I'm writing
passionately
about my love for others.

You don't see me
when I tear up
while reading the saddest—
and happiest—
parts in a book.

You don't see me
when my eyes light up
at the sight of a new place
I'm seeing for the first time,
or the view of the world
when I reach the top
of a structure I've been
climbing.

You don't see me
as I weep
while reading the news.

You don't see me
as I face my fears,
wipe my own tears,
and take on the world
another day.

You have painted your picture
of dark skies
and prickly thorns,
of poisonous apples, and
a ravenous villain.
But you don't see me
dancing under a rainbow sky
hoping that one day
everyone else can too.

In fact,
you don't see me—
you've never seen me—
at all.

Is it Clear Yet?

•••

These tattoos on my skin
were not inked there for you.
The jewelry in my face
was not pierced there for you.
These lashes I wear,
the way I color my hair,
the paint on my toes,
and my choice of clothes…

The lip fillers I want,
the body I flaunt,
all of the things that I do,
I don't do them for you.

You don't even cross my
mind,
not one single time,
when I look in the mirror
or slide on my heels.
What I'm doing for me
is not about how you'll feel.

I don't need your approval,
your opinion or permission
to decorate my body or
choose my own image.
I don't care if you like it
or think that it's *sexy*,
whatever I choose is not
because society *lets* me.

Your views about women
are about their appearance,
but you think we bash men
when you're acting abhorrent,
and you don't offer a single
perspective that's important…

Trust me when I say,
women don't give a fuck
what you think.

I Left Him in Pieces

•••

I only wanted peace.
Still, he viewed me as a piece

of meat

A body to give him release
And now I have to leave his body

in pieces.

Slash. Slash.

Chop. Chop.

It's never enough to say no.
Still we are being told

our bodies are not our own.

With my knife,
I thee stab.
They don't rape
when they are dead.

Slash. Slash.

Chop. Chop.

Another piece
of human filth,
Another fetus
that should have been dealt

with.

What if that fetus
could have cured cancer?

What if that fetus
grew to rape your daughter?

Slash. Slash.

Chop. Chop.

Take the pieces,
bag them up;
My peace is ruined,
this night is fucked.

I only wanted peace,
to be left alone on the
street;

instead, he will have to leave

here in pieces.

I Live in the Fire

●●●

They threw me in the fire
and laughed while I burned.
They said that I deserved it,
by destroying me
others will learn.

They demanded my loyalty,
to use my femininity
as they wish.
They never expected me
to fight back,
extract my claws,
use my fists.

And so it took many of them
to wrestle me down,
though they stripped me bare,
I still wear my crown.

And as the fire is fueled,
the gasoline spilled,
my diamonds are sparkling
my heart over filled.

They may burn my body,
though my heart will still rise.
They may bury me
beneath the dirt,
though they can't take my pride.

You will hear them call me
many hateful things,
though it was their hate
that cut off my wings.

And when I return
and sprout from my cocoon
I will not be a butterfly
or a flower in bloom.

For I am a warrior
an undying threat
and we will fight on
until they regret
the burdens they have
used to weigh us down,
the stones they have thrown
till we fell to the ground.

My ashes shall scatter,
and then I shall rise
just like the phoenix,
soaring the skies.

I will not perish,
I will not die;
my strength will live on
forever in fire.

No Weak Woman

•••

Let them dig my grave,
I already feel dead.
Until they take me out,
I'll chop off a few heads.
Kicking and screaming,
watch out, I'm teething.
I won't go down
without a fight.
They call us the weak ones,
the damsels in distress.
But their anger and hatred
got us into this mess.
Sharp objects,
quick wit;
we aren't done yet.
You get the gasoline,
I'll grab the matches.
Whether them or us,
one will turn to ashes.
We will snarl and bite
until we are free.
They may write my ending,
I will write my eulogy.

The Villain

•••

I'll be the villain in your story,
the wild, untamed beast.
I will rage with fire and fury,
I will bare and sharpen my teeth.

I will be the villain
that you hunt,
degrade,
and regret,

though you are the creator
of the monster
that you met.

You miscalculated
when you called us witches.

You underestimated
the power we've been given.

You claim us weak,
though you're still afraid
of the damage we can do
with all of this rage.

And so, I'll be the villain,
the dragon,
the troll,
because I've never been good
at doing what I've been told.

The Problem with Religion

•••

The problem with
religion
is not that they believe or
pray,
it isn't

The problem with
religion
is that they will use it
against you
as soon as you make
a mistake
as soon as you are
different
as soon as you don't fit
in the box that you were
given

As soon as you
don't follow the
rules,
as soon as you love
every one,
as soon as you
translate a verse
different
in their Bible
they think their god
has written

As soon as you help your
neighbors
and make your table a little
bigger,
as soon as you respect
all love
as soon as freedom
is coveted

You see,
the problem with
religion
is not prayers, or thoughts,
it isn't;
the problem is in their
aversion
to help
and strive
to listen

Only in *cults*
do we do as they say,
as in religion
your voice has
no sway

When it all started
we wanted to believe
in greater, in better,
in eternity

Though the problem with
religion
isn't hope for
ever after,
the problem with
religion
is the leaders,
yes, the pastors
who make kids believe
their very soul
is on a path of
disaster
if they do not
follow suit
if they do not allow
men to choose
if they do not love
the opposite gender

and form a family
in the church of
tradition

Religion itself
is all rules
and regulations,
a deadly map
to guide us away
from temptation

All we want
is to love who we love
help those who struggle
and believe
in whatever god
or goddess
above

But religion isn't
freedom
and choice isn't
free
when you use
religion
to control
humanity

Wild Women

•••

I do not dance naked
under the moon.
I do not use voodoo
to control what men do.
I do not read tarot or palms
or minds.
I do not chant spells or use magic
to hide my crimes.

I'm not plotting revenge
on those who have wronged me.
I'm not holding grudges
against those who have shunned me.
I'm not brewing potions
of frog sweat and blood;
I'm not sacrificing men…
though, maybe I should.

I'm not growing a garden
of thorns with no rose.
I'm not scaring the children
with my long, crooked nose.
I'm not transforming my enemies
into black cats who talk,
and I'm not riding a broom
when I can easily walk.

But if they could burn me
there on the stake,
they would claim me a witch,
evil and crazed.

For women just
should
not
be
outspoken, assertive,
or ornery.
Women shouldn't
be so proud.

Amanda L. Ball

Women shouldn't
be so loud.

Women like me
aren't witches at all;
we are the descendants
of the brave women
men hung on the wall.

No,
I don't need witchcraft
or dolls poked with pins,
because Karma, the goddess,
is my life long friend.
She is always there
watching my back,
she feeds me gut feelings
and keeps my soul on track.

I do envy Karma;
she always wins.
She is the "witches" they burned
again and again.
She is back for vengeance,
here for revenge;
I'm simply her voice,
unafraid
of standing up to them.

They never hunted witches—
who seek harmony
and peace;
they trapped and burned
women
who they couldn't keep
in line with their rules,
their control, their
religion;
they want us to believe
that *our* sins
are different.

Maybe I *will*
dance under the moon.
I'll take my black cat
and my cauldron too.
I'll howl at the stars,
chant a spell or two;
maybe Karma will join me—
she's a wild woman too.

Enchanted Forest

•••

I took a walk into the forest
to try to clear my mind,
to try to calm my heart.
The trees—and leaves—called to me
in the whimsical way they waved
like art.

The path looked bright and cheery
from a distance where I entered.
As I crossed the threshold,
my soul felt more centered.

Though, as I traveled further in,
I saw a storm was brewing.
But as I turned back to leave,
the path was already closing.

There was no way other than forward,
and I felt so much strife.
Am I strong enough to weather this;
will I make it out alive?

…

As I ventured deep inside
of the forest's trees,
I stumbled upon helpless creatures
hiding under leaves.

They glared at me with fright, as
they shook and they shivered,
so I scooped them into my arms,
ensuring to safety they'd be delivered.

As my new friends and I
continued further on,
the clouds turned black and
lightning struck, and we
calmed our nerves with a song.

As our voices echoed out
through the forest's path,
our melody called to other creatures
who were afraid they wouldn't last.

So we invited them on our journey,
and I promised to see them through;
for I had strengths they had lacked,
while their knowledge of the forest
would help guide us too.

And so we journeyed on,
humbled in this storm;
for as we worked together
and used the forest's charm,
we would come out stronger
and keep each other safe
from harm.

Eat the Rich

•••

Hungry. Starving.
Searching for our next
feeding.

Picking up scraps
while they sit in their towers
laughing at us
while we turn into beggars.

Keeping clean their
pure white gloves
while us animals down here
are covered in blood.

Lying and mocking us,
watching us grovel
as we fight and quarrel
and blame one another.

The people are desperate.
The people are famished.
The people are getting sick

of all the games they use to
control us;
it's time to
eat.the.rich.

Grab your weapons.
Take up arms.
Stampede together.
Break down their doors.

Climb up to the tower top,
there's no better time than
this
to take back what they stole
from us;
it's time to
eat.the.rich.

Storm of Enchanted Dreams

It is okay to rest.

Enchanted Dreams.

Stardust

• • •

Our souls are formed from stardust in the universe

and yet

we are fighting over money and power and greed;

excuse me for a moment while I go back to the stars

I will return soon to fight for peace.

The Wishing Well

•••

I took a journey
to the wishing well

I threw in a penny
just to tell

my wish
for me
my wish
for you.

There's a dragon
in the wishing well
She demands a price
and a penny
just won't do.

I needed to drop
my wish into
the well
to see it swirl
to watch it
swell.

I begged and I bartered
I turned out my pockets
some little morsel
to please her
some little token
to appease her.

Now I can see
the dragon is me
protecting me
from myself.

And so, I turned to leave
and said…

I wish you well.

I Remember the Girl

•••

I remember the girl
who used to be scared
who tip-toed around
others' feelings
afraid to lay bare
her own sadness
for fear no one cared.

I remember the girl
with her shy, quiet smile
who followed the rules
and suffered all the while,
as she never voiced her needs,
for no one listens to a child.

I remember the girl
who felt never enough
whose hair was too straight
who wasn't very tough;
she hid in the shadows
when life was too much.

I remember the girl
who never said no
who wanted to please
and put on the best show
who held herself back
from being able to grow.

I remember the girl
who lost her sweet smile
whose world was uprooted
when her father died.

I remember the girl
with built up rage
who could no longer be quiet
who could no longer be caged.

I remember the girl
who chose big dreams
who left the past
ripped at the seams.

I remember the girl
with fire in her eyes
who lived how she pleased
and didn't apologize.

I remember each girl,
each version I have been;
I wish I had loved
each one back then.

Now I'm growing into the woman
I was always meant to be;
I can't fucking wait to meet her
and allow her to fully be Me.

When She Played with Barbie

•••

I'm feeling all the nostalgia…
here I am writing songs
spilling my heart out
in my bedroom
lights off

Listening to Taylor
hearing all her words…
like she's singing
my songs
like she's reading
my thoughts
like her heart
is my broken heart

I'm feeling all the nostalgia…
reminiscing about
my young heart
when all the words
she wrote
spoke of so much
soul

How did she ever know?
Just how deep did she go?

When I still believed
fairytales weren't
make-believe
and Barbie would never be
alone…

When dress up
was safe
When there was
no place
where loss was
real
and where I could
feel
forever
[brave]

I'm feeling so much
nostalgia…
when my only drama
was which dress
and shoes
to place on
my doll

But still her heart
knew
she had been
through
so much more
in another life
before

For how deep did she go?
How old was her soul…

When she still believed
in make-believe
in fairytales
in wishing wells
and Barbie never needed
to sleep

An Endless Puddle

•••

I wept the tears
I kept holding back
and I fall into a puddle
of my own sorrow
of my own making

I formed a stream
I could easily cross
but the storm hasn't
yet passed
so I added stones
I could hop across
but the puddle was
growing fast

I tried to stop it
I swear I did
but my eyes would
not oblige
for all these years
I held them back
I couldn't stop them
falling as I cried

I cried for her
the girl holding pain
I cried because she never
knew it was okay
to share her sadness
with the world
so afraid it would
leave a stain

I wept more tears
that could fill
a lake, a river, an ocean
now I might have to swim
before I stand again
I've never felt so open

I cried for the girl
who felt less than
I cried for her aching heart
I tried to tell her I love her
but she couldn't hear me
through all of the hurt

I've built a bridge
so that I may walk
or crawl
the tears I weep
won't let me keep
my balance
and I fall

I cried for her
the girl who was scared
afraid to live loudly
freely
too afraid to ever dare

I'm swimming in this
downpour
or am I drowning after all?
Maybe if I build a dam
this will come to an end
only, there is one flaw

No wall could be so tall
no barricade so strong
to stop these tears
held back for years
now they're falling where
they belong

There are oceans of sadness
there are rivers of pain
and in this puddle
I see her there
staring me right in the face

She is finally smiling
She has been set free
the tears are gone
she is strong
and she's so fucking proud
of me

Escape

•••

I want to escape into a world
where hate is not an option,
where forgiveness isn't
necessary,
and greed is all forgotten.

I want to escape into a world
where all life's creatures are
respected,
where murder is unthinkable,
and
animosity is unaccepted.

I want to escape into a world
where *all* people are accepted,
where love is love, colors are
equal,
and anger is redirected.

I want to escape into a world
where science drives
decisions—
not religion, or wealth, and
definitely not opinions.

I want to escape into a world
where weapons are not
needed,
where hope is never lost,
and dreams are not impeded.

I want to escape into a world
void of fear and doubt,
vacant of obstruction,
where no child goes without.

I want to escape into a world
where love is all I'm craving.

I want to escape into a
world…
a world that is worth saving.

Stuck in a Dystopian Dimension

•••

I am not made of sugar and
spice
I do not exist
to simply be nice

My soul craves justice
My heart craves peace
But my mind is fueled
by the inequalities
of this so-called democracy

Such an angry woman,
like they know me so well
They don't know my burdens
They haven't seen my hell
And I do not have to walk in
it
to carry it like a shell

The pain of others,
The sorrows of many
It doesn't have to be personal
For me to see that they matter

As empathy dies on the hill
they have built
humanity cries, and writhes,
and wilts

This is not a dystopian story
I've written
This is the life—the world—
we've been given

My soul was meant for
softness,
not fury,
but I was not created
to be judged by their jury

I yearn for a world
that doesn't exist,
a utopian dimension
better than this

The Girl You Used to Know

•••

Say goodbye to the girl
you used to know;
the girl who said "Yes"
and rarely said "No".

Say goodbye to the girl
who lived to please,
the girl who was desperate
to fill her need
for love and attention,
for a place to belong,
for people who praised her...
to be seen as strong.

Say goodbye to the girl
who only saw her worth
if someone else gave her
a reason to first.

The girl has grown,
the girl has changed.
The girl you knew
is not the same.

The girl has fallen
more in love
with herself.
She no longer
needs approval
from anyone else.

Garden Growing

•••

Cozy and nestled
in the dark soil,
I feel comfortable
here.

Water comes,
a sprig is formed,
I like this look
on me.

Daylight is here,
I feel the warmth,
I yearn for it
on my face.

I want to sprout,
to come out,
but I am so cozy
in my space.

All of the flowers
surround me,
blooming without
a care.

My stems aren't ready,
my leaves feel heavy,
and my petals feel
out of place.

More water comes,
it feels like drowning;
I know I need
the care.

But I would rather stay
tucked inside,
protected, warm,
and safe.

I want to bloom,
I want to grow,
I want to flower
and change.

But night has come,
the day is done,
and I am still
the same.

Maybe tomorrow
will be my day,
my time will come
to be on display.

I see all the
other beauties
showing off their
growth.

When I see them
all shining,
I feel totally
alone.

Down here
in the dirt,
I must admit
I've lost hope.

But I keep accepting
the nurturing
and looking out
for the sun.

For one day,
I know,
my growth
will come.

And I will
keep changing
and growing
into more,

because that's
exactly
what life
is for.

Keep Your Light

•••

I hope that when you're little
you're made to believe
you can be anything
you want to be.

And I hope that when you're
older,
and you grow and you
change,
that you don't let the world
take that away.

I hope you still sing
at the top of your lungs
and twirl in circles,
dancing under the sun;
I hope you still play
and kiss your stuffed animals
goodnight.

I hope the world
doesn't drain you
of all of your light.

I hope you can laugh
and smile
amongst the storms;
I hope that chaos
never knocks at your door.

And when life happens
and you trip and fall,
I hope love is there
to pick you up...
or help you to crawl.

Immersion

•••

Plunge me down into your ocean
and wash away my fears.
Engulf me fully in your flames
and burn away my tears.
Propel me forward into your atmosphere
so your gravity keeps me steady.
Soak me lavishly in your stars
so your light guides me when I'm ready.
Submerge me deeply in your energy
and allow me to share your power.
Bury me firmly in your garden
so I may bloom and flower.
Plummet me distantly into your galaxy
so I may transcend your time and space.
Drench me unsparingly in your clouds
so I may wallow in your embrace.
Embed me lovingly into your ink
so I may climb inside your story.
Pour me freely into your drink
so I may nourish your body.
Douse me elaborately in your fragrance
so I may always smell brand new.
Cover me wholly in your leaves
so I may stay wrapped up in you.
Inundate me profusely with your sky
so I may soar in your breeze.
Bathe me completely in your light;
let me shade you with my trees.
Shower me tenderly in your downpour
so I may rinse away my doubt.
Absorb me adoringly in your love
so I never go without.

Patchwork

•••

Open me up
slide inside
look around
and you might find
the patchwork of
emotions, thoughts,
ideas
I keep tucked inside
my mind.

Strip me down
remove my clothes,
vulnerable and bare,
I'm now exposed
for you to view
the patchwork of
ink, art, stories
I choose to keep
so close.

Meet me in
another place
even for a moment
to get just a taste
of the patchwork of
adventures, beauty,
journeys
I have chosen
to face.

Speak to the ones
I hold so dear,
the ones who know
I *do* have fears;
you will then find
the patchwork of
friends, confidantes,
supporters
I choose to be near.

Listen to my stories
read the poems I write
get lost in the words
that feed my appetite
with the patchwork of
struggles, memories,
angst
I keep locked up
so tight.

My patchwork skin
and patchwork mind
make up the pieces,
places, people
I have left behind;
like a sticker book,
my patchwork life
is a beautiful patchwork
but it is wholly mine.

The Soul's Plight

•••

When you were little
and you looked up
at the sky
and you wished on a star
that one day
you'd fly,
did you ever believe,
imagine, or consider
that your soul
was much more
than the body you were given
here on earth's floor?

I believe, as children,
our connection is stored
inside our minds
as we dream and envision;
maybe one day
that can all be restored.

If only we could all retrieve
the hope and wonder
we once conceived,
but alas,
we move too fast
and dreams are only
make-believe.

I dream of one last chance
to lick the bowl,
lick the whisk
while my granny giggles
at my mustache made
of batter mix.

I dream of running
through the garden sprinkler,
one last leap
before family dinner,
catching fireflies
in my palms,
watch them light the night,
oh, so calm.

I miss when monsters
were under my bed,
not out in the street…
or in my head.

I miss when "sweet dreams"
was a simple "good night",
not a desperate plea
for a restful night.

The soul holds on
to so much more
than we see,
than we know.

The soul becomes heavy
as we grow older,
it's not just our hair
that is turning greyer.

The colors are slowly seeping,
washing away,
like hopscotch on the
sidewalk;
now no one wants to play.

Oh, let us be little
one day again;
instead of playing Red Rover,
letting nobody in.

Red Light,
Green Light,
Simon Says…
I really just want
to believe
I can fly again.

Clue.less

•••

My soul is but a candlestick
burning flame, lighting my way
through the library of endless tales with
words thrown into a wishing well

And as the flame burns brighter
it extinguishes just as fast
and I am left in the dark
with a dagger in my back

Crawl to the study to write more words
as I rope them into my pages
dance in the ballroom until I am
wrenched of all my anger

Take a break within the kitchen
as the revolver stares me down
try to drown out all my worries
in the billiards room I found

Down the hall to the conservatory
lead pipe in my hand
resting on the sofa in the lounge
seeking light again

Searching through this clueless house
with my clueless mind
dodging the ghosts and demons
clueless that they are mine

Entertaining My Musings

•••

I entertain my musings,
swish them around
in my mouth
and spit them out
onto the page.
I color them
in dainty words
in colors of blue,
and yellow,
and red,
and grey.

I entertain my musings,
playing them each
like chords of a
violin.
Strumming the words
like
Do-Re-Mi-Fa-So-La-Ti-Do
as they fall
from the ink.

I entertain my musings
sending myself
on mindless—or mindful—
adventures…
and chaos.

Word vomit.
A mess.
A chaotic mess
of a chaotic mind.

And still
I entertain
my musings.

It's the Pieces

•••

It's the pieces.

The pieces of a pie
delectable with every bite

The pieces of the sky
that break as clouds roll by

The pieces of the moon
that sometimes show and hide

The pieces of the trees
elongated branches and misshaped leaves

The pieces of a quilt
patched up and woven through the seams

The pieces of a memory
fragmented in time

The pieces of a life
I have made truly mine

The pieces of my soul
I'm learning to find

It's the pieces. The million little pieces
that make up my mind.

My Mind's Drawing Board
• • •

It starts with words.

My mind is an
                    endless
                                    place
        of words
                and ideas
                    endless love
                        tortuous sadness
                            unwanted anger
                                hopeful desire

A bucket
        pouring
                    out
                        all
                            the
                                    content.

SLAMMIMG
        into the pavement
            s c a t t e r e d
                    b-r-o-k-e-n
                        b R u I s E d

My mind is a
        torrential
            D
              O
                W
                  N
                    P
                      O
                        U
                          R

        gushing rain
                    heavy winds
                        ↓ umbrellas
                            drenched ↑
        soaked clothes
                    on a soaked
                            BoDy.

My mind is a
      HEAVY burden
            a weighted iron
                   gLuEd
                       to.the.floor

My mind is a
      ROLLercoASTER
           drifting UP
                 DRIFTING down
        loOPiNG and SwOOpiNG
              ʊ aROUND and
                     aROUND

My mind is an

             island…

                   alone at sea…

My mind is an
      OCEAN…so vast…so…
              oPEn, so…
                  CLoseD

    swimming like fish
Back
                  and forth.

My mind is a
      ROCket
          sh oo ting
             into the SKY
    B U R S T I N G in fLAmes
        as it reaches
            new HEIGHTS

My mind is the
        painter
           my bOdy
             her cANVAs…
               drAwInG my stoRIes
                wriTing my bOOk

My MIND is the
        ARTIST
            Me?
                only the
                     BRU
                     S
                     H

And it ends with words.

Her

•••

She is fire
She is love
She gives freely
She doesn't budge
She walks proudly
She stands tall
She isn't afraid
to be wrong
She is sexy
She is plain
She cries oceans
She feels pain
She is fierce
She is proud
She isn't afraid
to be loud
She encourages
She supports
She is an ally
She is a force
She is calm
She is a storm
She isn't afraid
to break down doors
She speaks up
She holds back
She loves in color
She loves in black
She walks alone
She lets people in

She isn't afraid
to get hurt again
She dreams
She wanders
She lusts
She ponders
She runs
She stops
She isn't afraid
to get lost
She cries
She shares
She hugs
She dares
She hopes
She wishes
She isn't afraid
to ask questions
She is beauty
She is hope
She can heal
She can cope
She is strong
She is brave
She. Isn't. Afraid.
I am her,
and she is me.
She is proud of
who she chose to be.

Imperfectly You

•••

I want to encourage
the old and the new
I want to forge paths
for love to brew

I want the gay children
to know they are already
enough;
I want the "theys" to always
feel loved

If she becomes him
or he becomes her
I want them to feel safe
I want them to be heard

I want all the children
who love boys *and* girls
to know love has no limits
you're allowed to love plurals

I want all the differences,
oddities, and uniques
to know they have a place
in this world;
they deserve to be seen,
for being the same
isn't all that it seems

I want all the outcasts
to feel inspired,
for where there is hate
there is space to transpire,
to show your strength,
to show your fire

I want the children
who may feel different
to know they are not
required to fit in

There is no box
for your shape,
there is no set path
you have to take

You are enough
just as you are;
you are fully human
and we all have scars

Close the apps
turn off the news,
the hate is blatant,
the hate is abuse

But you…you matter,
your heart and dreams too;
you are perfect,
Imperfectly You.

The Mind's Visitor

•••

You leapt across my mind today
and sat down in the corner.
You waited there while my day moved on,
but I noticed you lingering on the border.

A smile crept in as you sat in my mind,
but, alas, it quickly passed,
as you were overshadowed by
the day's worries and stress.

I took a moment to step away
and there you were again,
hopping and skipping across my mind
like having coffee with a long lost friend.

You aren't in there every day,
but you love to make surprise visits,
sometimes reminding me of a silly moment,
but then sometimes the sadness hits.

You are the best cloud inside my mind,
hovering, waiting to pour,
even though I prepare my umbrella,
I'm always left wanting more.

Sometimes you're there, inside my head,
even after I ask you to leave;
how am I ever supposed to move on
if you won't let me be?

Other days I'm glad you're there
making me laugh out loudly,
for the jokes you shared
I used to find corny,
you always told so proudly.

You leapt across my mind today
and I watched your big, bright smile
light up my head and heart,
and I asked you to stay awhile.

Word Art

•••

Words are my bricks
that build up a house.
They are all the thoughts
that never leave my mouth.
Words are my stars
that light up the sky;
they are all of the dreams
I fall into each night.
Words make me feel things
I can't even explain;
like thunder and lightning,
words are like rain.
Words give me comfort
when my heart is a mess.
They guide me through heartbreak
and pull the pain from my chest.
Words are an adventure
with battles to win.
They open up places
many have never been.
Words can build castles
and tell me fairytales are real.
They help me climb mountains
and show me dragons can be killed.
Words can bring power
but they can also bring pain.
They can fill up your mind and
they also contain
the strength to bring
people together,
or even the potential to make
a relationship sever.
Words are wrapped deep inside
the paint strokes on
a beautiful painting.
They give us hope
and keep us thinking.
Words are like rare gems
buried deep in a mountain.

Words are all of the mistakes
that I keep counting.
Words give us direction,
they give us a name.
No two words
are exactly the same.
Words can bring us to our knees;
they can also warm our heart.
Words create every single thing.
My words are my art.

Perfectly Imperfect

●●●

I have loved.
I have been loved.
I have been let down.
I have let others down.
I have said powerful things.
I have said the wrong things.
I have encouraged.
I have needed encouragement.
I have been laughed at.
I have laughed at others.
I have made mistakes.
I've been someone else's mistake.
I'm a hero in some stories.
I'm a villain in others.
I have been right.
I have been wrong.
I have been up, on top of the world.
I have been down, in the depths of despair.
I have given help.
I have needed help.
I have picked others up.
I have tripped and fallen.
I have made some of the best decisions.
I have made some of the worst decisions.
I have called myself beautiful.
I have called myself plain.
I have made myself unique.
I have tried to blend in.
I have been agreeable.
I have disagreed.
I am all of the things I have ever been.
I am nothing I was before.
I am me.
I am adapting.
I am growing.
I am never finished.
I am aware.

When Girls Dream

•••

Stories say that girls dream
of their wedding and ponies.
They dream of gifts of
flowers,
especially roses.
I'm told that girls dream of
the love of their life,
of creating a home for their
family, of being a wife.

These are the dreams
I heard and believed,
but luckily I learned to
love to read.
Reading is brave when
you don't read what you're
told.
Reading shapes minds…
it made me bold.

So let me tell you the story
of what girls really dream of.
While love is involved,
it's not all about love.

Girls dream of flying,
adventures, and freedom.
Girls are *not* dreaming of
the day a man will leave
them.

When girls dream
they see passion and fun.
They're leading the next
group of
women into the sun.

Girls dream dreams bigger
than fairytales say.
Girls dream that tomorrow
they'll get their way.

Girls don't dream of
screaming kids, runny
noses—
sure, some probably do…
but when girls dream,
they dream of a life
better for me and you.

When girls dream of what's
yet to come,
it fuels the fire of work
still to be done.

Girls can dream dreams
of success and goals
bigger than any
storybook shows.

When girls dream,
they can rule the world.
So go after your dreams,
and never stop dreaming,
brave girl.

Satan is a Woman

•••

Maybe this war between
woman and man
started with the gods,
and the devil is a woman
cast out, shunned,
and lost

Stripped of her wings,
sent to a fiery hell,
much like the witches
whose stories
we know so well

Satan, the woman,
the outcasted rebel,
overpowered, tortured,
and sent to her dwelling

While all of the people—
the women, the children—
were told of her evil,
and frightened into
believing

Though Satan,
the goddess,
the powerful queen
takes in all the outcasts
and helps them feel seen;
she mothers their wounds,
and wipes clean their "sins",
accepts them for who
they have always been

They call god "He"
and it's become so clear
that man has wanted control
of women for years,
for decades, generations,
since the dawn of time;
if you don't do as they say,
you will pay for your crimes

But what they won't tell
you—
the outcasts, the sinners,
the rebels, the gays—
the mother, Satan,
is the one who
will accept you
and love you
and won't cast you
away

And So She Roared...

•••

They caged her
to control her
and set soldiers
upon her

They hunted her
stalked her
called her a beast

An unnatural woman
with no respect for man
they could not allow
her to be freed again

Bound tightly in shackles,
bronze metal chains,
as she scratched
and she clawed
and they called her
unhinged

Stripped of her clothing
stripped of her pride
doused in cold water
nowhere to hide

They called her wicked
a monster,
a witch,
anything at all
to make her sound
less
human

They turned her into
the wild animal
she is
when they
sewed tightly
shut
her lips

It took many men
to wrangle her up
while they caged
her body
she is so
much

more than the bones
connected inside her
more than the blood
that runs through her veins

She is not timid,
mild mannered,
or weak,
but a lion(ess)
just on the brink
of becoming the very
animal
they claim
her to be

Locked in a cage
more time to think,
more time to plot,
more time to see
all of their moves,
all of their minds,
the little games,
and all of their crimes

So she decided
to play their game,
to make them think
she *was* weak

Oh, the poor damsel
is in distress
she needs food
she needs rest

And so she gained
their trust
once more
and waited
patiently
for her time
to score

They made her the
animal
she has become
they made her the
monster
that kids are scared of

They caged her, sure,
but tame her, never,
and they underestimated
just how clever
and smart
and angry she was

But if they wanted an
animal…
that's what she would become

So, she smiled sweetly
when they opened the door,
acted quite weakly
as they climbed in
on the floor
she lifted her head,
sad eyes no more,
and with all of her breath
and anger
she

ROARED.

It is okay to dream.

Her Story Continues

•••

Chapter 7:

She did it again
packed up and moved on
climbed in her car
with her tiny, precious dog
and ventured out to see more sights
to live an uncertain
nomadic life.
From city to city
she met people who
would teach her, show her
so many things new.
She piled on the miles
and paid for the gas,
she planned for more
as she drew on her maps,
but the body—and the mind—
grew weary,
exhausted, stuck,
a hopeless ending.
And so, she ventured
one more time
to settle into a place
where she would find
the friends—the women—
her life was missing.
Even mishaps can have
happy endings.

Chapter 8:
She is turning forty now,
and life has kind of slowed
her down.
She had fallen into a
monotonous routine,
wake up,
clock in,
sit down,
and dream.
As one chapter—one era—
comes to an end,
she is building her strength
to be inspired again.
All of her words
written in ink,
typed up, re-worded
as fast as she can think.
That lifelong dream
of that once little girl
who at one time saw
all the hope in the world,
she was buried for such
a long time
and now she is daring
to come out from hiding
to share her words,
to share her grief,
to share her passions,
to find her peace.
After so much pain,
and too many losses,
she is starting a new chapter
and this is where her story
pauses.

What comes next
even she doesn't know,
but she hopes to inspire
just one lost soul.

My heart is too soft for this world, my mind too vast, my
soul too fierce.

• • •

May every dreamer fight through the storm for the healing
and love you deserve and always follow your dreams.

Bonus Ending (first edition)

Happily Ever After
•••
Fairytales and lullabies
got me through many
sleepless nights.

Whether Grimm or Mother Goose
there were so many lessons
and paths to choose.

Rock-a-bye baby
and Miss Muffett
carried me into my dreams…

Some nights I was Humpty
up on the wall
never feeling scared
that one day I might fall.

Then just like Alice
I'd slip down the rabbit hole
shrinking and growing
my heart battling my soul.

Other nights I was Belle
in a magical library filled with words
getting lost in all the pages
of all my favorite books.

I could be a mermaid
or I could be the Queen of Hearts
then turn into a dark clothed villain
baking poisonous apple tarts.

The nursery rhymes and lullabies
and all the fairytales
taught me that magic exists
inside wishing wells.

I could be Rapunzel
locked in her high tower
waiting to be rescued
not knowing she always had the power.

I have slipped into dreams
both in night and day
I've never stopped believing
that dragons can be slayed.

Though white knights are only make-believe
and ruling men are cowards
as they hide behind their soldiers
locked inside their dark towers.

Witches aren't the evil ones
and princesses don't need saving
by a man on a horse
who thinks she is his reward for the taking.

No, the princesses and witches took care of each other
building a forest of furry friends, fairies, and laughter
and in this storybook

she lived

happily

in her dreams ever after.

P.S. Magic does still exist. Keep looking up at the moon. ☾

First Edition Epilogue

I wrote every one of these poems after packing up and leaving my home state at 35 years old and prior to turning 40, hoping this book would be published before then. *Her Story* in the beginning of this book introduces you to who I was up to that point. Then, I wrote my heart out while I lived, while I cried, while I begged for relief, while I learned about myself so much more, while I healed, and while I have been pursuing my lifelong dream. *Her Story Continues* brings you to where I am as I type these words. I am very much looking forward to a new era, a new decade.

Since I was a child, I have always written poetry in a way that feels whimsical in my head, my heart, and my hand. Rhymes—Dr. Seuss, Mother Goose, and Shel Silverstein—were my favorite as a little girl. Rhymes have always felt melodic to me. Since I cannot sing the songs I write, I shall turn them into poetry.

I grew up on nursery rhymes and fairytales, and I never stopped believing in magic. I hope you never do either.

Here's to following your dreams no matter your age.

The villain can always be defeated. Dream big!

• • •

Second Edition Introduction

My writing will always be lyrical and playful. I want to inspire the adults of the world to not stop dreaming as you age. I forgot that for a while. So, I am back now reminding you that once upon a time, you too were a child with big, hopeful dreams, wishes running wild, licking the whisk, running through the sprinkler, waiting for Santa to deliver the wonder.

Please, don't forget, magic really does exist.

May you enjoy these witchy dreams.

♡ Amanda
(a.k.a. The Book Witch)

The Dream Witch.

Fairytale Beginning

•••

I tried to imagine
a life in the clouds
with white picket fences
and quiet, peaceful towns,
where neighbors were friends
and monsters were few,
where little girls could grow
to do anything they wanted to
do

But the storms rolled in
driven by villains,
the kind who believe
they are the victims,
and the poor, lost souls
get poorer,
while our planet dies
and the rich get richer

To be young again
is to dream of better,
to believe there is no
hardship you can't weather;
and believing that love
and friendship is all that
matters

Though, as we have grown
into a middle age,
we see all the greed,
we are buried in hate;
our words are not heard,
our screams are silent,
locked in our minds
of torture most violent

Children go hungry,
while women are killed;
men call us crazy
and break down our will;
and still…
we encourage children
to believe in fairytales

Fairytales are full
of wicked storms,
of toxic apples,
and the prickliest thorns;
and yet we keep expecting
a happily ever after story

They make us out
to be ungrateful sinners,
and use their god as a ruse—
their weapon of religion,
to guide the lost to believe
every fable that they deliver

In every storybook
it is quite clear early on,
which side is corrupt and
evil—
which side is wrong;
and we all must choose
which side to fight on

History repeats,
stories re-told,
yet so many can't see
that they are being conned;
just like the Trojans,
tricked during the war

If you still believe
in fairytale endings,
then you must know
it is only the beginning
of a story when the
villain is winning...

So, we must fight through
this chaotic storm;
we must brave the bombs
and the wind tunnels formed,
and remember that
this story
is only
just
beginning

Won't You Join My Coven?

•••

The Evangelicals are out
again,
claiming Catholics are all
sinners.
And then the Baptists are at
my door,
pointing fingers at other
Christians.

They are all demanding
we abide by their book,
but they don't even give us
the time to look
up the rules and
requirements—
special policies in the fine
print.

Another pastor
charged with crimes
against more children…
when their innocence died.

And still they claim
their book the truth,
their god the greatest,
His fury true.

So is He mad?
Or is He loving?
Are we made in His image?
Or are we abominations?

I'm still waiting
for someone to explain it.

Do as they say,
not as they do.
Speak ill of the outcasts,
don't speak your truth.

It was religion that killed
women—not witches.
It is preachers—
congregations—
abusing their children.

They shall not spew their
bible at me;
their words fall flat at my feet.
I do not need religion
to tell me that my soul is
different…
I can *feel* it.
I was made for something
bigger.

I do not yet know all the
spells,
or the ingredients for potions,
but I do believe
the moon chose me
to travel solo on my
mission—
to help the other women,
to fight for all of those who
are different,
to prove friendship is not
missing.

No, I will not join their cult—
their religion their existence;
I will seek you all out,
the lost souls who almost
drowned,
and I will pull you back to
safety,
encourage you to keep going,
for we do not trust a god
to save us from this peril.

We only have each other,
in this war against women.

So, tell me, are you in?

Won't you join my coven?

Our story can now begin…

Seeking My Coven

•••

Once a solo witch without a coven,
looking within, outside, and above me
for just a hint—a glimpse—
of purpose, of belonging.

Beneath my feet, the earth it roots me,
above my head, the moon swoons me,
and in the air, the wind moves me,
while deep inside my soul, fire fuels me

as I seek out calmer waters to soothe me.

Trapped inside an endless cycle,
I do not ask man's god to guide me,
I only ask for my coven to find me,
forever my soul to keep
as they *fiercely* protect me.

And as the moon cycles
and the earth circles
around the sun
another year done
I have watched the days tick on,
the years, they blend,
another decade gone;
loss of loves, of friends, of hope,
aching to feel like somewhere is home.

I am not sure that I was made
to stay rooted in one place;
I crave somewhere with open space,
so that I may feel Mother Nature's embrace.

I call out to the solo witches,
the wicked women
who crave endless friendship;
oh, won't you join me in my mission—
a community we can all belong in.

I seek you out,
and so, I shall find
a coven of friendship
that is truly mine.

In Between

•••

The ground beneath my feet, moving me;
gravity above pushing me,
rooting me
down.

The clouds above my head, guiding me;
the ache in my soul, battling,
claiming me
destroying me.

The sun in the sky, warming me;
the moon at night,
as I dream,
comforting me.

There is an ache in my bones
taking over me,
reminding me
I am here for only
a brief
moment,
a glitch in time,
ending instantly.

The dust floating by in the wind
covering me,
the ghosts of my past
enveloping me
wholly,
haunting me
slowly.

When my body returns to the earth
will there it remain;
or will my energy escape
gravity
and finally
be free,
floating?

For now, I am stuck
here
in the
in between,
waiting for...
something,
or someone,
to notice me
clearly,
beautifully,
completely.

Until then, I'll keep dreaming.

Magic Wand

•••

If I had a magic wand
I'd make pain go away;
no child would go hungry,
no person would feel hate.

My friends would be filled
with happiness,
not the overwhelming burdens
of capitalist stress.

More people would frolic,
and less would yell;
there would be no religions
sending people to hell.

We would love ourselves harder
and laugh so much more;
greed would be condemned,
the rich would help the poor.

If I had a magic wand
we wouldn't go to sleep at night
dreading another day of work—
the endless cycle of life.

We would all be free to embrace
life as we were meant to—
more days to enjoy
as we choose to spend them.

Maybe some days
my head is in the clouds,
but I refuse to let hatred
tear people down.

I *can* dream of a better world
where we would all belong…
knowing what could truly be,
if I had a magic wand.

Treehouse Castle of Dreams

•••

I am not trying to build a legacy,
a brand that goes down in history;
I am not trying to seal my name
into any fortune or fame.

I am only building a place…

A space in the clouds that I can climb to,
where I can escape back into
a childhood dream of fairies and queens;
where we don't kiss the frogs
or wish for a prince;
we just wish for happy endings for friends.

Where witches aren't the evil ones,
and man is seen for what he is.
Where women tame dragons,
and are not forced to have kids.

A place high in the treetops
where I still believe I can fly;
and I get to sleep beneath
my blanket moon each night.

Where all of the little girls
are safe from boys who are mean,
where women are treated
with the highest esteem.

That is all I'm building here—
a treehouse of wishful scenes;
where anything can happen, girl,
anything can be,
when you are living in
a castle of dreams.

Surviving the Storm

•••

Following the rules
made by man
is how we lose
our independence.

The trolls demand more
to cross their bridges,
even though the poor
are the ones who built them.

The sick are denied
life-saving treatment,
cancer and disease
claiming more victims.

Our planet is burning
while bombs are exploding,
and we keep being told
the innocent deserved it.

And still, we fund it…

The rich could end hunger
with a wave of their hand—
pennies to them—
and improve our land.

But greed drives man…

And there are still women
gripped by their spell,
women who think
they are safe from our hell.

But monsters help no one,
they take and they take;
they show no pity,
they feed off of hate.

And so we must all awaken
to the truth of the world;
these men can't be trusted
to protect little girls.

In the battles,
we must all partake
to survive the storm
in our wake.

Rock-A-Bye Lady

•••

Rock-a-bye, lady, in your comfy chair
when the world outside is too much to bear
when the bills come quicker than the funds
and the chores and dishes still aren't done

Lady, you're drowning, it's plain to see
but your resilience is admirable as can be
forward and backward, feels like you can't win
though, you are endlessly loved by your friends

Rock-a-bye, lady, take time to rest
a nice, hot bath, a cool compress
a book you can escape into
and remind yourself to keep pushing through

Rock-a-bye, lady, straighten your crown
do not let the patriarchy get you down
for when morning comes, the sun will rise
and you'll need your rest to keep up the fight

Fascist Fire of Ice

•••

The world is burning
as we watch,
as we bleed,
as we keep working.

Clock in, take calls,
attend our meetings.
Pretend we aren't drowning,
pretend we aren't feeling

all of the pain,
the anger, the hurt,
as we watch them lower
children into the dirt.

I wish empathy *was*
a made-up word—
leftist propaganda—
not a jagged sword

stabbing my guts
as I scream out in pain;
are we truly meant
to live this way?

Wake up again,
breathe the air.
Turn off the news;
it's too much to bear.

Right and left—
it will never end,
as long as racism,
greed, and hate
continue to win.

I envision a meadow
with a peaceful stream,
a place where children—
and adults—can dream

of a world where people
aren't "illegal,"
of a space
where bombs of fire—and ICE—
have no place.

Still, we are always expected
to get up early, to attend to our duties.

I have never met another soul
who wishes
for this suffering
existence.

Instead of bathing in flowers
inside a field,
we are making money
to just pay bills.

Our children are dying
inside their schools,
inside their churches,
inside their homes.

And on the tv, they hear
the president say
they aren't welcome here.

And so, they're ripped
from loving arms,
separated from parents
who can no longer protect them
from any harm.

They place their hands
on top their bibles,
uttering passages
they don't even believe in.

They twist and turn
those sacred words
to make them fit into
their box of choice.

Religion is a dead-end street,
filled with guns,
with murder,
with infidelities;

and yet,
those who hold empathy
are met with more
hostility

simply because
we demand equality;
we demand
peace.

I wish I had more time to write,
time to dream—even time to fight;
but alas, I must get back to work…
the fascists demand I pay my worth.

Do Not Fear the Dark

•••

Fairytales often tell us
women need to be saved
by brave, white heroes
expecting to be praised.

Though in this fairytale
all women matter,
and men are defeated
while glass slippers shatter.

Women have blossomed
from quiet and meek
to taking down men
who think we are weak.

And with our minds
and compassionate hearts,
we will teach new generations
to not fear the dark.

For women are more
courageous and bold,
and we are no longer
doing what we are told.
We will climb the towers
where they are hiding—
afraid of the power
we have trapped inside us.

And we will rage
as we defeat;
and in our victory,
they will meet

the ferocious women
that they have denied
their rightful place—
locking us outside.

And though we may stumble
we shall not fall
because
we will pick each other
right
back
up.

The Big Bad Witch

•••

It was not the big, bad wolf to fear,
but the witch who fought back
when they came for her.

They hunted her through the forest's trees,
disguising themselves as innocent and sweet.
But the witch, she knew, not to fall
for the ruse they've been re-using all along.

We have learned to sniff out their lies and crimes.
And we refuse to allow more women to die
at the hands of evil men;
and so, it is *our* turn to trick them.

Lure them out into *our* woods;
feed them from our basket of goods;
and when they turn sickly and pale,
reveal to them our true selves.

The big, bad witches do not take kindly
to men who refuse to leave us quietly.
Our boundaries no longer negotiable,
we do not accept men's toxic offers.

Lessons from Freddy

•••

I said "No"
and you heard "Not yet"
and this is why I've turned into
a nightmare you won't forget.

We choose the bear
because men are weak,
because you can't leave us alone
out on the street.

I will not smile.
I will fucking scream
if you even attempt
to fucking touch me.

And then I will make you bleed.

You stand no chance
in your fucking dreams.

Freddy taught me where to hide
inside the dark, inside your mind.

I will stalk you in your sleep,
watch you writhe as you dream.

I am the nightmare that comes for toxic creeps.

I will be prowling outside your eyes
as your story unfolds in your mind.

I will be pulling all the strings.
That is what Freddy has taught me.

Revenge Bath

•••

As little girls, we were fed stories
that convinced us
a white knight
would one day save us.

And so we waited for our
Prince Charming,
expecting a happy
fairytale ending.

And too many women
accepted abhorrence,
beratement,
and torture

just so we could
finally
be chosen.

And though we saw it all
with our very own eyes,
we still refused to realize

that men are not swooping
in to save us;
and their hatred of women
is so very blatant…

and still, women accept it.

They'll call us man-haters
when we fight back;
they'll call us evil
when we attack;

though *they* are the reason
this war is upon us;
and they are now
our open target.

Their importance has dwindled
and they need someone to blame,
and we have finally been let out
of our cage

that *they* chained us up in…
now wanting praise
for allowing us freedom.

And they still question
why we don't trust them.

I guess they should have
thought about that
before they made us their victims.

And still they expect us
to act like a princess;

though they have turned us
into the villains,

and revenge is what
I choose to bathe in.

Not even their god can save them…

Macabre Nursery Rhyme

• • •

One, two,
my blood stain
knuckles are bruised

Three, four,
I knocked him to the floor

Five, six,
stomped on his dick

Seven, eight,
dug his grave

Nine, ten,
at peace again

Eleven, twelve,
sent him straight to hell.

Crazy Cat Mom

•••

I love you in the morning
when you're bouncing off the walls.
I love you when you're mischievous,
and when you're bapping with your paws.

I love you when you're gnawing
your razor sharp teeth into my skin.
I love you when you're knocking
all my things down with a bang.

I love you when you're climbing
and scratching on things you shouldn't.
I love you when you're driving us
all crazy with your antics.

I love you when you're talking back
and always telling me no.
I love your fire energy
and all of your tiny bean toes.

I melt when you are sleeping
and I finally get some peace.
But I love you fiercely and endlessly
because you trust that I'll keep you safe.

While I'll be thankful for the quiet
when you grow and calm,
I love every little sassy bit of you,
and I'm so grateful I'm your mom.

The Fate of Humpty Dumpty

•••

We all know the famous nursery rhyme
that told us of Humpty Dumpty's demise;
all the king's men
failed to put him together again,

and that is where we thought it ends…

Humpty was not a good, kind soul.
He spread his wrath wherever he would go.
He demanded more and took and took;
in front of our very eyes, we saw the crook.

His noblemen stood by his side,
protecting all his vicious lies.
The people watched it all from outside
and knew something must be done to make things right.

And so they sought out the witches,
requesting a spell or curse to grant their wishes.
Though the witch understood more than most
that evil, powerful men who boast and boast

will not go down without a fight,
and so she mixed a tincture with much delight,
gave the people clear instructions
for how to use this magic potion.

The witch would lure him to the top,
promising jewels and magic that he could flaunt;
that is, right after the kitchen staff
slipped the poison into his mash.

Humpty Dumpty was already weak,
for he was far too old to be running things,
and so it would be an easy task
to have him wobbling in no time flat.

As he enjoyed his view from the top of his kingdom,
his vision got blurry and he felt quite weakly;
but he could not see past the riches
promised to him by evil villains.

And as he reached for the shiny power,
he tumbled down from his tower;
as all the king's horses and all the king's men
ran to put him together again,

the people took the opportunity
to reclaim their power, as was their duty
to the future generations,
by removing the tyrant king without hesitation.

And so, you see, Humpty Dumpty deserved his end,
as he could not put aside the pride and evil inside of him
to be the leader that the people need;
no, we were not born to live like sheep.

A Tired Old Witch

•••

I stare at the cinnamon stick
tied there to my broom
above my door
in my main room.

I know it's old
and should be replaced,
to welcome abundance
into my space.

My crystals aren't charged—
I missed the full moon;
therefore, plain tap water
will have to do.

I haven't pulled a card
from my tarot deck in months;
I don't have the energy
to eat healthy—just junk.

I fall asleep at night
with good intentions
to do more tomorrow…
then I forget to do dishes.

Some think being a witch is all
curses and black magic spells,
that I spend my days crafting pure evil
to send my enemies straight to hell.

But I've reached middle age,
and I don't sleep so great.
I'm just a tired witch
who can't even remember the date.

For all you tired witches
who feel how I feel,
just remember that witchcraft
belongs completely to yourself.

Set your intention,
do the best you can,
and once we've all had a nap,
we can try again.

The Magic of Youth

•••

I remember digging treasures
right out of the ground,
doing cartwheels in the grass,
and laughing so loud.

Riding my bike
hands in the air
without any worry
without any care.

Making up stories,
sharing secrets with friends,
pinky promises,
and wishes again and again.

Being a kid felt magical.
I could believe in anything.

Living like Snow White
with all of her friends;
falling in love like Belle
with her beastly prince.

Riding dragons
and unicorns,
Barbie cars
and wicked thorns.

There was magic in movies,
magic in books,
magic in stories—
everywhere I looked.

And then I was made to become an adult.

And the world took my magic away.

Paying bills and making dates,
thinking I need a prince to be saved.

It took some time
to see the light,
to remember the wishes
I made each night
beneath my glow-up stars
on my ceiling, in the dark.

That little girl saw beauty
in so many things;
she didn't need much
to go adventuring.

A little imagination,
a sprinkle of wonder,
a few good friends,
and some animal comfort.

I've discovered
wisdom comes with age,
and I have finally
turned the page.

I am much wiser
than I was then;
and as you get older
you can see the magic again.

A Cursed Woman

•••

Little miss priss
was told she was too much—
too loud, too bossy,
too smart for her own good.

As they tried to
tone her down,
she kept rising
from the fucking ground.

As she carved out
her own life,
not needing a man
by her side,

they claimed her
a lonely old maid,
warning children
of this fate.

That is why they all
now stay off her lawn,
afraid of the curse
upon her home.

And inside her cottage
alone with her cats
she is grateful for peace
as she enjoys her nap.

Not Your Womb-an

•••

They demand our bodies
demand our energy
to grow their babies
and raise their family.

They are denying medicine
that can help women choose
claiming us murderers when
we don't see a pregnancy through.

They judge us for choosing
not to be moms
but still refuse to help
all the children along.

They are only pro-birth
not pro-life
they do not give a fuck
if children thrive.

They also don't care
if children survive
allowing more guns
to end their lives.

He says he wants children
and that white picket fence
but he is not putting
the same effort in.

Single mothers are the norm
as men just walk away
judging every choice she makes
as the mothers are to blame.

When we say we don't want children
they cry, oh why, oh why
and say we'll change our mind one day
or we'll have a wasted life.

So, ladies, if you choose to
become a mother or not
you will be judged either way
that is what we are taught.

I say fuck the societal norms
I will do what I want to do
and for those who disagree
I am not the womb-an for you.

The Wicked Witch of My Dreams

•••

They called her a villain,
a wild, untamed witch,
spread lies about her and
told stories with which
they claimed she held evil powers
right inside her hands;
and warned the little children
and all of the land
that her fury was boiling,
and she was seeking out men
to sacrifice to her gods
as she lured them right in.

The people were not certain
where these stories began,
or where she came from—
this man-eating woman,
as she lived alone
inside her cottage,
surrounded by animals
and a wealth of knowledge.

Little did they know,
she found her peace
within the woods,
covered by trees.
She built up her library
and her kitty coven
(and very rarely placed
men in the oven).

She started those stories,
that is her secret;
weaving dark, whimsy tales
knowing they would believe them.

This gave her the freedom
to do as she pleased,
as men left her alone
after she made them scream.

No, she didn't eat children—
they turned out not-so-tasty;
but on occasion she did bathe
in men's tears (when they called her crazy).
She basked in her peace,
sharing her time with friends,
not worrying about how
her story would end.

That woman who built
a life all her own
was never, ever
truly alone.
She scripted her vengeance
and laid out her schemes
in the pages of her fables—
the wicked witch
of her very own dreams.

A Happy Ending

•••

Okay then, fine,
I will tell you a story
not filled with anger,
or gore, or fury.

I will cook up a tale
of a sweet little girl
who discovered love
so true and pure.

No evil stepmothers
holding her back,
and never, ever
blaming dad.

I will weave a fable
of all her fancy dresses,
of her magic library,
and all the frogs turned
princes.

I will craft a script
of a once-little girl
grown up to be a princess
and handed the world.

Where all the king's men
ride in on white steeds;
and no man would ever kiss
a lady while she sleeps.

I will write the words
that give you a hopeful heart,
that tell us that life
will one day give us all we
want.

Just make your wishes
as you blow out your candles,
and your dreams will
transform
into your wildest desires.

This story will not
remind you that
life is hard
and dangerous.

This little tale
I choose to tell,
will remind you of
true love's spell.

As long as the beast
says he's sorry
and promises never, ever
to yet again harm you,

then he can be trusted
to become your
Prince Charming.

I can dream up
a happier scene,
where animals talk
and men aren't mean.

I am most certain
I can find
the words to tell
of a fictional life

where girls are rescued
by older men
who see how mature
they are for their age.

Oh, I promise
I can write
a fairytale
of a beautiful life.

Please, just let me
check my notes,
and find the ideas
to craft a happy home.

A father, a mother,
two beautiful children,
living happily
ever after

with their dog and
white picket fence,
and plenty of food
for all the kids.

It must be possible
to spell out—
a life we're all taught
to dream about.

It is there
in my memory—
girls being saved,
the prince always winning.

I may need more time
back at the drawing board
before a happy ending
can be formed.

Dream Sweetly
•••

I enjoy the sunshine
on my face,
I enjoy the flowers
in bloom;
though as the day
melts away
I am grateful for
the moon.

She is a tinder constant,
a comforting
hope,
providing guidance
and extending
a hand
when I struggle
to cope.

And through my
window—
the looking glass—
I wish on the
stars
as they
pass.

And I smile at her,
and she at me,
for we have been
friends
for an
eternity.

She knows all
of the secrets
that I keep
and she accepts
me for me.

She sees me grieve,
she sees me weep;
she watches over me
as I sleep,

so that I can sweetly dream.

Master Peace

• • •

That little girl is smiling
as she consumes all of the words
as her heart bleeds
and her tears burn
rolling down her cheeks
as she reads her master peace.

Fairytale Ending

•••

She wrote down the last word
and set back with a grin,
proud of her work
from beginning to end.

She flipped through the pages
and patted her own back,
reminding herself
to never hold back.

It would be easy to fret
about others' opinions,
but she weaves her stories
how she wants to tell them.

It may not end
with a true love's kiss;
though she does kiss her cats
each night before bed.

She spends her free time
doing whatever she chooses;
she answers to no one,
she picks her own music.

When she is tired,
she takes a nap,
sometimes alone,
sometimes with her cats.

She reads many books—
gets lost in the words;
she goes to bed at night
knowing her worth.

There is no partner
to help—or hinder,
no one to fight with
over what's for dinner.

She looks forward to the time
she spends with friends,
vowing no man will ever
tell her what to do again.

In her earlier stories,
she saved and she helped,
never placing her empathy
away on a shelf.

Even when it was hard
to make ends meet,
she gave back to others
in their time of need.

She faced her own demons
that followed her around—
made them her confidantes,
and made herself proud.

While she is now in the middle
of her very own story,
she reminds herself
not to be in a hurry;

for one day she will write the final chapter
of which she's been dreaming—
as she has the power to script
her own fairytale ending.

It is okay to believe.

Final Bonus Ending

The Dream Path

•••

You are on a walking tour in an old library.
It is small and the path is narrow.
There is only one way you can go to reach the other side.
It is dark and musty—no electricity or light.

It's really old.
Dust lines the books and shelves—
books long forgotten, but you mustn't dwell.
Your first thought is to get through the path as quickly as you can—
it shouldn't be much further now—right?
The end is just up ahead.

Finally, the path opens up.
More room to breathe.
More to see.
Feeling less stuck.

The others go on ahead,
you're meant to follow—
behind is dread.

And then you remember
the stories you read
of hidden passages—
hidden rooms and doors

tucked into the
shelves of books—
perhaps you'll go back,
have a look?

You search and you search,
through the dust and the dark,
almost giving up hope—
rejoining the pack.

But then you discover
your strengths,
your sixth senses;
try once again,
search every corner.

And sure enough,
a hollow sound—
as you placed your heel—
there—on the ground.

Another tap,
now a dance,
it's like your soul
knows the steps.

And there it is,
a creaky door—
a grand adventure—
another world.

It awaits you
up ahead,
stay the path,
forge ahead.

Watch for fallen branches
and snakes in the leaves;
carry a torch if you must,
whatever you need.

Help the others
on your path;
stay weary of strangers,
but always give back.

Seek out adventure
at every turn;
live your life open
to all you can learn.

You will make it
because it was you
who chose to veer off
into another room.

You do not have to take
the clear path laid out ahead;
you can choose a life
that isn't full of dread.

If you become lost
or down on your luck,
if you begin to feel weary,
begin to feel stuck

remember the girl
who always believed
she could do and be anything
she wanted to be.

The End. (for now)

Storm of Enchanted Dreams

A Note from the Author

I chose to write a second edition of *Storm of Enchanted Dreams: a poetic fairytale* for one main reason, and I believe it's important enough to address it here, especially for those readers who purchased book one, supporting my lifelong dream. In my day job, I work in technology, and AI is a hot topic these days. AI can be helpful to allow many of us to do our jobs quicker and more efficiently, giving us time back in our day to focus on things that truly matter. I knew I had to embrace AI as a new technology tool if I was going to survive in my line of work. As a new, indie author with limited resources—just a lifelong dream—I utilized AI to create the original cover photo on my first book.

Although, since releasing that first book and connecting with other authors and creatives, I have done the work to learn more about the harm of AI. I am not here to persuade anyone one way or the other, as it is easy to learn more about and decide for yourself. I have chosen to honor and respect all the creatives out there. AI steals work from talented, everyday people like authors and visual artists. This second edition is a remake of that original cover photo with the help of a human artist redesigning it in their own way.

I am proud of the work I put into that first edition, but I am even more grateful to know that I can continue to learn and grow as I age. I hope each of you choose to keep an open mind and to allow it to expand when new facts are presented. I do not fear new technologies, but I do know we can choose to use them in a way that does as little harm as possible to living, breathing humans and other creatures.

I hope that this re-release corrects any wrongs others may have seen in my first edition and gives you hope that we can all become better than we were yesterday. Thank you for trusting in me and for supporting my dream.

I hope you now go chase your own enchanted dreams.
♡ Amanda

P.S. I hope you enjoy the following sneak peek bonus content for an introduction to my new book, *Witches in Wonderland: a poetic adventure.*

SNEAK PEEK

An introduction to *Witches in Wonderland: a poetic adventure*

The Dream Witch: Wickedly Ever After

•••

Now I lay me
down to sleep,
my soul to rest,
so please don't weep.

I battled demons,
and almost drowned.
What I had lost
could not be found.

I walked galaxies,
I fought the dragons—
those I could see, and
those hidden in shadows.

Fueled by fire
inside my soul,
my light almost out,
no longer feel whole.

Going to bed each night
manifesting a dream land
that I could fall into,
not to awaken again.

A peaceful slumber—
all I craved,
not this hustle,
this weight,
the burdens,
the graves.

Just like Alice,
I kept awakening
knowing that the magic exists
in another place,
on another plane.
Finding my escape—
getting lost in a book;
turning pages too fast—
to get to the good.

I want to read the ending,
I want to know the answers.
I don't want the hardship,
the fighting,
the distance.

I just wanted the
happy ever after.

Instead, I found
the haunted woods,
the bears in houses
I sought for food.

I met the wolves
who bore their teeth,
waiting for their time to
strike—
to take the meat.

I saw them blow
the houses down—
those made of straw—
not rock or stone.

I saw them laugh
as the piggies scattered—
as they screamed, and bled,
as their lives shattered.

And the wolves
built castles—
such powerful structures,
while they threw
the piggies morsels,
with no paid lunches.

I walked the road—
made of yellow brick.
I danced with lions,
with tigers,
with bears…
I allowed them to
guide me
into their lairs.

I begged to see
behind the curtain;
I pleaded,
I wished,
I hoped,
and I screamed.

I cursed the man
inside the moon—
his face a reminder
of a long ago youth.

A little girl
grown up too soon.

I searched for the witches
inside the forests—
offered to lure the children,
so they could teach
while I learn.

I basked under the moon—
I never felt freer.
I steered myself
toward fun…
and danger.

I made deals with the devil,
and met the underworld
goddess—
she had it all,
the beauty, the grace—
she was my karma.

I convinced the emperor
he had on fancy robes;
pulled him into my spell,
only to leave him, unclothed.

I fought alongside
Robin in his hood—
taking from the rich
to give to the poor.

I fed the starving children,
while I cursed evil men.
I saved all the creatures,
while I hurt some close
friends.

I thought those old bruises
of that long-ago girl
meant she deserved
a payback—of sorts.

I turned into the villain
staring into the mirror—
on the wall—in my tower;
believing I deserved
to hold all the power.

I weaved my web,
I lured in my victims;
I scattered my hurt
like it was seasoning.

I understood villains—
in the light—
in the dark.
I began to appreciate
their macabre art.
I hooded myself
in a silky, red robe.
I searched for my
granny
in the stars,
in the woods.

And when I needed
to find my way home,
she would protect me
from the monsters;
she would never
leave me alone.

I nuzzled up into
Papa Bear's lap,
asked him for
just one
more
story
before I take my nap.

Just one more chance
to watch them laugh
to watch them dance.

I begged to them—
please, bring me home.
Don't leave me here,
I can't do this alone.

I watched the princess
grow up too soon,
I watched the evil
lock her in her room.

In her mind
she dreamed up
a place
where dogs play
in rainbows,
where little girls'
daddies are safe.

Where kids don't
have to
grow up too soon;
where you can
always
wish on the moon.

Where genies are
brought
right out of
a lamp.

Where magic is real.

Where fireflies dance.

Where every miracle
comes from my hands.

Oh, she dreamed so big,
that long-ago girl,
of magic mermaids,
of a unicorn world.

So if I shall not
tomorrow wake,
do know that I
am in a place
where little girls
are writing
on their beds
in their rooms.

Where little girls
sleep under the stars
inside the moon.

I'm stirring up villains,
writing the scripts;
to give the next little girls
some dreams
and inspiration.

For good and evil
are the same—
on the same seesaw—
up…down…again.

And so, mama,
don't worry,
if your little girl's soul
leans a little bit dark,
a little more bold.

Your little girl has fire
deep inside her bones;
she will one day awaken
to all the power
that she holds.

And she will be okay
after you're long gone.
She will make her way—
as she's always done before.

You can rest in peace
knowing she is strong.
She has always carried
mountains—
in heels—
in the snow.

Yes, they call her a rebel,
but if you look deeper, still,
you will find that her heart
is three sizes too big.

She carries it all—
she writes it all down;
not always on paper—
some thoughts lost,
never found.

Maybe she will rise like
Gretel—
overturn the villains
to free the children.
Or maybe she will be Snow
White—
surrounded by friends—
by the forest—
by light.

Maybe she will fall,
like Ariel swooned,
in love with a man
who will give up too soon.

Or maybe she will dance
like Beauty
in love with her beast,
in love with his fury.

Maybe she will get lost,
like Rapunzel—
in her own stories,
as she's locked in her tower.

Maybe she will obey,
like Cinder-elly.
Maybe her [fairy] godmother
will grant all her wishes.

May her prince—
who is charming—
never make her sleep
on a pea,
just to prove her worth,
just to be believed.

May she not fall into
a spinster's trap,
never fall into a deep sleep
in an unknown bear's lap.

May she explore
the seven seas.
May she bring kings
to their knees.

May she rise
more than she falls.
May she always
heed her own calls.

May she follow *every* dream.

May she become the heart
fit for a queen.

May she follow a rabbit
down into a hole.
May she not always do
what she is told.

I will plant these seeds in
their heads.
As you tuck them into bed.
Read these words
as they go to sleep.

I promise all
of their secrets
I'll keep.

I will nurture their minds
of possibilities—endless;
I will teach them of love.
I will teach them of
vengeance.

I will teach them courage—
unlike the lion;
I will teach them of
the real-life tin men—
the ones with no heart—
the ones who are lying.

I will teach them of witches
who might eat little
children—
but if you get to know them,
they're actually sweet, like a
kitten.
I will teach them of
adventures
out on their own—
not next to a man,
but next to a coven.

I will teach them that animals
deserve more love than
humans,
but we should never forget
to help all of the children.

I may feed her a darker tale—
of huntresses—starving—
turning predator on
the evil monsters.

Slithering through the trees—
like a snake—
beady eyes
waiting to strike.

Of course, I'll tell them,
"not all men",
but many
many
many
many of them.

I will teach her to
go for the throat.
With her claws
with her teeth
with her soul.

But I will also bring her
out of the dark—
a nice, cozy place
under a blanket
by the fire.

A memory of wishing
up on the stars
and believing that she
can fly up to Mars.

Reminding her
there are no limits,
there are no milestones
or goals to hit.

The only goal
is to stay alive—
to dream of a night
filled with fireflies.

To remind her to not
grow up too soon.
To always say "yes"
to dancing under the moon.

To remind her to cherish
every laugh with a friend,
every tear,
every celebration.

To honor the moments
where she feels most alive.
To always tuck herself
in at night.

To show her that there is no
"right way";
to ensure she always
stands in her place.

To help those behind,
even if it's a little—
it's not such a burden
when you've already
had dinner.

To light up the world
with all of her fire,
with her breath,
her soul,
with her earthly desires.

To believe in a world
much better than this.
To remind her she never
has to have kids.

She can be whatever
she chooses to be—
a wise old witch,
run an apothecary.

Or that white picket fence
she can also choose—
that is, if
she really wants to.

But I will not let her forget
that her path is her own—
not mine, and not yours.

So read her the tales
of the witch who grants
wishes—
inside little girls' dreams—
not inside kitchens.

Where Alice is waiting
in a room full of cats,
surrounded by books
as she slips into her naps.

Pulled in by
a queen gone mad,
ready to chop off
every traitor's head.

I might weave fables
of chilling with caterpillars
wrapped up in their arms
when my head's a bit hazy.

This is the job of the Dream
Witch,
you see—
the girls dream what they
want,
believe what they choose to
believe.

I hope every single one
in every galaxy
in all the universes
in all the minds
in every star—
on every moon,

knows that they hold their
own power
they know their own truth.

That there will always be
other girls out there
who will have what they
need.
Friends are the essence
of life, dear girl—
friends hold the key.

Love who you want,
but always lift
other girls up.
Pour into others,
but don't drain
your own cup.

If we allow them,
they will win—
pitting us against
one another
to control us again.
I am here to tell
the secrets that are
tucked away—
hidden well.

The tales of lists—
that don't exist—
of evil rich kings.

The tales of women
rising up
standing in
their power.

She may go home
each night
to slip into bed
with him

but she will always
be reminded
of who and what
she has always been.

As she closes her
lids each night,
I will greet her
in the light.

Guide her through
the forest
down the dark path
to remind her of
the witches' past.

To ensure they never forget
that long ago
witches were our friends.

Before man wrote the stories
that turned them into
crooks—
burned at the stake
for knowing their worth.

For seeing their magic
built right inside,
before we were cursed
into a menial life.

The spell can be broken,
it says in this book;
so come closer,
dear girls,
come, have a look.
Fall asleep each night
tucked in by the moon;
may you never have to
grow up too soon.

And if your soul—and
heart—
is a little bit darker,
may you always dream
wickedly
ever after.

Love,
The Dream Witch

For the mama bears.
And the witchy women.

To be continued…(in *Witches in Wonderland: a poetic adventure*)

About the Author

Amanda L. Ball has been writing poetry since she was a young girl, having her first poem published in a book for young poets at age 11. It has been her lifelong dream to publish her own collection of poetry. She is a loud, relentless voice for social justice and cares deeply about child and animal welfare.

Though she grew up and lived in Texas for 35 years, she has spent time traveling the world, living as a nomad across the country, and currently resides in the state of Maryland with her four cats, enjoying her passion for books and writing, and reveling in the middle-aged friendships she has discovered, grown, and continues to nurture every day.

And she has never stopped dreaming.

• • •

Other Works by the Author:
Wicked Dreams Goodnight: a witchy fairytale
Witches in Wonderland: a poetic adventure (coming soon)

Follow the author on social media: *@echoendlessmind*

www.ingramcontent.com/pod-product-compliance
Lightning Source LLC
Chambersburg PA
CBHW060417130626
46555CB00005B/2095